From Bridges to Big 'Uns
A Sort of West Side Story

P.J. Coster
C.Eng, MICE, MCIT

No.46254 CITY OF STOKE ON TRENT with a down express, a relief to the Midday Scot. She has just cleared Grayrigg Bank and is accelerating towards the Lune Valley and Shap in August 1964.

Irwell Press Ltd.

Copyright IRWELL PRESS LIMITED

ISBN 978-1-906919-88-7

First published in the United Kingdom in 2016
by Irwell Press Limited, 59A, High Street, Clophill,
Bedfordshire MK45 4BE
Printed by L.F. Bokkservices, UK

Contents

BR Class 5 No.73040 gets to grips with Camden Bank with the ECS of an overnight sleeping car service in 1963.

Preamble

This book is a collection of memories, experiences and anecdotes from one who joined the London Midland Region (LMR) of British Railways (BR) and trained as an engineer, mainly in civil engineering, with that organisation. The book is set out chronologically and it is not intended in any way to be an exhaustive description or history, because my acquaintance was far from comprehensive. Beyond Crewe that acquaintance, apart from cab riding, reduces to a handful of locations almost entirely concerned with bridgeworks or, later, photography. My involvement in the electrification project work gives the narrative a southern emphasis. At one time I was responsible in the Divisional Civil Engineer's organisation for permanent way (p.way) renewal, then maintenance on the Euston-Shilton and St.Pancras-Oakley sections, which means that I knew the routes well in the 1960s. On the other hand bridge works, new works, schemes and surveys tended to be location specific. My site experience was gained during the electrification of the West Coast main line (WCML), and the work involved with that enormous change is woven into the narrative.

Memories of the LMR would be incomplete without reference to the days of steam traction. Before I started work, my knowledge of the old LMSR was confined to occasional visits to Willesden and Cricklewood depots, uninvited, as were those of many of my generation. My knowledge of the timetable and operating practice was virtually nil in 1953, and while I learnt a certain amount, I was – and am still – far from expert. I have described events in my career as I saw them, as accurately as my memory allows after nearly 60 years. Some stand out, such as my first sight of the old arrival platforms at Euston on my first morning, but the details of others are less clearly recalled. Journeys during my first five years were opportunities to sample the performances of Royal Scots, Patriots and Jubilees and, most sought after, Sir William's magnificent Pacifics – the Big 'Uns or Big Lizzies as some Camden footplatemen referred to them. Timing trains and measuring speeds was a pastime of the day, stimulated by such writers as C.J. Allen and O.S. Nock. Therefore I have included a second part examining memories of operations and giving brief details of the more notable runs.

By 1961, the WCML had been flooded with English Electric Type 4s, equivalent to no more than a Scot, but unlimited by the fireman's shovel and capable of timing expresses to the schedules then in force. It had also been flooded with temporary speed restrictions (TSRs) for preparatory works for electrification and conversion to continuously welded rail (CWR). Performance was no longer interesting, but with the advent of better and faster colour film, the need to capture something of the passing steam scene had become urgent. Therefore I have reminisced photographically as it were, and included a selection of colour photographs. I make no apology for the emphasis on Stanier's Pacifics.

As a young schoolboy, my ambition was to be a steam locomotive engineer, but with the shadows of evening advancing towards steam traction, the future looked oily and electric. And so civil engineering beckoned as the future. During my 17 years with the LMR I met many good friends and learnt an enormous amount about the railway and its engineering. I remain in their debt. The narrative that follows might leave readers with the feeling that railway civil engineering was a juxtaposition of the hair-raising and the hilarious. As members of the media professions no doubt understand, work well done, unspectacularly, and results achieved on time and within budget do not often make news or call for remark. For much of the time railway engineering of all types continued successfully, at least until changes were made to established routines, sometimes without the appropriate planning and attention to detail. As in most activities in life, railway engineering has its language, and a glossary of abbreviations and terms is attached.

A working life of 40 years is a long while, and one has to choose very often between a fulfilling career and one devoted to the acquisition of wealth. It is a long while to be unfulfilled or just plain bored. BR trained people very well indeed, for not only did it encompass many different facets of engineering, but it had good and experienced people to teach and lead. It was an enormous organisation within which were many opportunities to vary or change one's career path. Quite a number of engineers in outside industry started with the railway. However, it failed signally in developing careers after training, and the rate of loss was around 95%, which no private company could tolerate.

However I remember fondly those colleagues, most now no longer with us, whose skills and experience made it a happy, instructive and fulfilling time. I look back without any regrets.

Barlow's mighty roof at St.Pancras restored to its former glory.

Time enough to photograph trains. Sedbergh station in 1964, and Ivatt 4MT 2-6-0 No.43035 waiting with a down freight.

Part I: CIVIL ENGINEERING
Chapter One: The Early Years

This course is intended to give you a thorough understanding of civil engineering. Be good enough to pass that knowledge on to others in due time. LJMMcS 1955

The scene is etched on my mind still, more than half a century later. On Monday November 9th 1953, I had started training as a student civil engineer at Euston, and made my way over the familiar GN metals into Kings Cross. The walk along Euston Road was new, and before starting in the office, I made my first close acquaintance with Euston Station. Entering the arrival side at Euston off Eversholt Street, there in platforms 1, 2 and 3 stood a stunning mighty triumvirate, a trio of Pacifics on the overnight expresses, 46239, 46245 and 46250, the CITIES of CHESTER, LONDON and LICHFIELD, together with Camden's 45735 COMET, one of the rebuilt Jubilees. It was my first sight of the main line LMSR in anger, a breathtaking and unforgettable one at that.

From then on, Euston was always inspected before doing battle with learning about structures, bridge repairs and renewals, and it was unusual in the morning not to see at least three if not four Pacifics lined up, waiting for the ECS

to be hauled out. In my experience the Pacifics on the overnights were always Big Lizzies, hardly ever the Lizzies, the earlier Pacifics. Almost always there was a Scot or one of the Patriot or Jubilee rebuilds on at least one of the other services. At lunchtime again there was usually a Pacific on one of the longer distance services together with some of the big 4-6-0s.

At the time the Eastern Region had taken on a full quota of trainees, so I had applied to the LMR, who sent a ticket, and welcomed me for training. It was a railway about which I knew little, but my luck was with me, as the southern part of the WCML was selected to be electrified under the 1955 Modernisation Plan. Not living on the route, not knowing the service and not knowing people involved in various roles in the operation of the railway meant that in the early years I felt out of my depth very often. Yes, a railway is a railway and much of the functioning and purpose was the same throughout BR, but one only has to think of the old

GWR to realise that within the constituent parts there are differences of practice, organisation and terminology which, although minor, are seemingly designed to highlight the stranger.

There didn't seem to be the same close monitoring by enthusiasts, at least in the south, as on the GN. However, it was the start of sixteen years spent working on the LMR, rather than the ER, the railway where I lived and with which I was deeply acquainted. In those years on the LM there were many experiences and memories, especially the first five years before steam was replaced by diesel and then electric traction. However, I do not claim a detailed historical knowledge of LM locomotives, nor much acquaintance with footplate and motive power staffs. As a civil engineer, the route itself was to become more familiar to me.

I started my railway career in the Bridge Office of the CCE's office at Euston. Euston Grove led off Euston Road, and passed under the former

The reconstruction of Bridge No.217 at Weedon with the pre-cast T-beams being placed together, in 1961. They will have been concreted so as to form a solid slab, but the pre-cast beams were not dead straight, and required caulking between beams to prevent loss of concrete. Subsequent removal of the caulking – usually tarred rope – was easier said than done! The abutments of the old bridge have been retained in brick to the new height.

The WCML equivalent of the ECML's famous Scots goods, 266 down, was the 14.10 from Broad Street (later Camden Goods), 4S68. The unnamed Britannia, No.70047, eases off approaching Willesden on 29 June 1964. The loco was known at the time as 'Six and seven eighths' on the basis that the Britannia names were drawn from a hat, and the last one left was the hat size label.

Euston Hotel block to reach Drummond Street and the Euston Arch. The office was to the west, before the hotel, and it was a temporary structure built of laminated timber on what appeared to be a bomb site at the west end of the hotel. The Bridge Office was at the far end. The Bridge Engineer was Frank Turton, a man whose appearance, with a dark suit and gold framed glasses, looked uncomfortably Germanic to a lad raised in the wartime years. He was in fact a pleasant man from the North Country, betrayed by his Lancashire accent, a man of few words but whose knowledge and experience I came to respect greatly. His assistant was Herbert Wyles, another North Countryman who seemed to do most of the communication with the sections.

I was allocated to the section led by Hartley Grunwell, who might have been a North Countryman originally, but had long hailed from the softer shires of Middlesex or Hertford, and was not far from retirement. A courteous and kindly old boy, he arrived, disrobed, and with an early cup of tea examined the *Daily Telegraph* closely and at length, with particular reference to the state of cricket and rugby. These were clearly matters of moment. By 10.00 tea was made, often by me, at which point Hartley would emerge from his glass box of an office, rub his hands and observe that it was a long day. Most of the direction and

advice came from his assistant, Gerald Humphries, expert, imperturbable and perpetually wreathed in blue smoke from his pipe. There were other characters in the section – Ron Jenkins, he of the immaculate draughtsmanship, Harry Humphries, another pipe smoker formerly with London Transport, 'Tach' , Eddie Nutt and Arthur Brown. Ron's work left me despairing, especially his printing, which was superb. Tach was Colonel Tachynovski, of the Polish armed forces, who settled in the UK, a clever engineer but who hadn't really grasped the language when I knew him. Arthur was a small eccentric North Countryman with even shorter, bandy legs and an almost impenetrable accent, who rolled his own cigarettes and kept a pair of ancient binoculars, (typists in Euston station for the observation of) and drank tea of the deepest umber. Arthur's frugal use of tobacco led to him smoking more paper than tobacco. The application of a match was followed by a sheet of flame and half the cigarette gone! In days when pencils were sharpened, a bogus cigarette loaded with pencil sharpenings had been left for Arthur, with fairly spectacular results!

Across the way was the section led by Jack Thorne. His assistant was 'Tiny' Vincent, a big man and another delightful eccentric. A good engineer, Tiny was in the habit of enjoying a liquid lunch, after which he would get a large plan out and pore over it. Snoring spoilt

the pretence, however. It was a favourite trick to ring him up from elsewhere in the office, and as he picked up his receiver, replace the phone. The reward was a stream of epithets. His section included some lively wits, and on one Christmas Eve when the drink had flown freely, as a result of a wager, one man rang the CCE's internal number 8400. This would normally have been intercepted by the secretary but no doubt she was out, and the West Country burr of Chief Civil Engineer A.N. Butland answered. ANB took few prisoners. The confidence of drink evaporated instantly. The caller, terrified, enquired *'Do you know who this is?'* ANB said something like *'Obviously not'*, to which the caller said *'Thank God'* and slammed the phone down. Later I learnt that ANB quite enjoyed the joke.

Behind us was Mr.Drummond's section. I had no occasion to deal with him, but Mr.D was by all accounts abrupt and rude, and not popular. In his section was Alex, another new boy, and Alex was keen on current fashion; long blue jacket, velvet collar and drainpipes. Mr.D was not, and was disparaging. It was not wise, however, to pick on young men, young men with the imp of mischief in their souls, young men who might realise that Mr.D's afternoon chocolate drink was the perfect vehicle for a well-known laxative. Mr.D paid a terrible price for his rudeness. I believe he never realised.

There was a small training section through which most of us passed, headed by the improbable figure of John Francis Charlesworth Heather. A large, tall man of considerable girth, his accent was a strange combination of Lancashire and German, a positive invitation to disbelief. There we were taught the rudiments of measuring up, booking and drawing, but it was good to get back to real work in the section. The graduates also passed through this section. I remember Ian Campbell spending time there, son of the former ER CCE, who rose to become Vice Chairman of the BRB and President of the Institution of Civil Engineers: I wonder what he made of it.

The Bridge Assessment section worked out the load bearing capacity of arch bridges from individual surveys, including details of cracking, distortion and wear. It was a sort of analytical guesswork. In the absence of a better method at the time, it must have been tedious, which perhaps explained why livelier minds broke the tedium with jokes. Brian Marriott, an Irish chap, and his Italian friend Tony (Antonio) were the stars. The discovery of joke dog's mess under his office chair caused Albert Jones, the venerable head of section, a nasty moment on his return from lunch. One of the most spectacular was on November 5th. While Tony was enthroned in the toilet closet, an 'unknown' hand rolled a lit firework from an adjacent cubicle.

I was surprised at first to find the extent to which the office rang with the sound of North Country voices. I gained the impression that the LMSR CCE's organisation was far more devolved than the BR version, probably utilising the pre-Grouping companies' organisations. The workshops and subsidiary offices were in the industrial Midlands and North. Periodically, meetings were held with the Area Resident Bridge Engineers (AREBs) together with the Works Manager from Newton Heath, the largest workshop on the Region. Afterwards they came round the sections to check on the progress of future bridge renewals. They were almost all from the north, good practical men and it was instructive to hear their comments on the designs. It was also interesting to hear the variations in north-western dialects. Newton Heath Depot (developed, I believe, from an L&Y carriage depot) produced most steel and concrete work for bridge and structural works, but with the advent of welding, private companies began to supply steelwork in greater quantities.

The other offices were concerned with Permanent Way, New Works, and Maintenance and General. The P Way office dealt with new S&C design, major realignment schemes, and standardisation matters. 'S&C' was Switches and Crossings, known to the laity as 'pointwork'. Assemblies of S&C were called 'layouts'. 'Points' was a term discouraged since it referred to a specifically shaped rail with a particular function such as a diamond point rail. The head of permanent way design was Albert Preston, and a spell in his office was essential to understanding the niceties of switch and crossing design, since Albert insisted on a high standard of work. On the District there were some older men who insisted on 'P&C' (Points and Crossings) as the correct term. This office also controlled the supply of quantities and regionally based plant to the Districts, the sub-divisions of the Region. New Works, as its name suggests, handled all forms of new work, other than the p.way, while the Maintenance office dealt with the major maintenance tasks that were beyond District capability, such as major tunnel maintenance, retaining walls, or the results of enthusiastic harbourside arrivals by BR's ferries! The offices had subsidiary sections, such as Heating Lighting & Ventilation, Outdoor Machinery, etc.

The Regional Architect was part of the CCE's organisation in those days. His staff were a colourful lot, with a profusion of beards and exotic clothing compared with the dark besuited CCE staff. One chap had an ancient Austin 7 restored splendidly in primrose yellow, which he parked prominently right outside the office entrance. I remember following the CCE into the office, and his glance at the vehicle was not one of admiration. The fair sex were not numerous in the office in those days, but one of the senior architects was a very tall Polish lady, who was regarded with more than a little apprehension by my senior colleagues.

Then there was the Staff Office, which dealt with personnel. It must have been a deadly place to work in. Whenever one went there, one felt the attitude was *We won't agree to it but what was it anyway?* In 1955 A.N. Butland took two places for student civil engineers on a new type of course known as a sandwich course, and I was selected with friend David Neale. This entailed studying at college during the winter months and returning to the office between times. The training system was not ready for this innovation, and we had the

'Jinty' No.47359 stands in the south bay at Stafford, with a new AC electric loco E3074 waiting behind, 1962.

Oxford Road station in Manchester. A producer of laminated timber in the Isle of Wight, I believe connected with yachting construction, pressed the Regional Architect to try the material. It was first used at the south end of Preston station, and Oxford Road was the first full-scale trial. It was bizarre in 1960s Manchester, and did not weather well. The laminated timber curved beams needed strap supports as can be seen, and the units tore along the laminations from the boltholes. A brave experiment. The toilets were tiled and the pattern used imparted a sense of disorientation which cannot have been helpful to late evening users!

impression that the Staff Office were making it up as we went along. Victories over the Staff Office were prized: when we went on the sandwich course we were told that privilege travel was suspended, but that was overruled by the CCE, bless him.

The other office we used was the Plan Room, which also did all the printing as well. There was always a whiff of ammonia from the Ozalid printing process. Some of the old L&B and LNWR plans were superb, leaving my colleagues and I with a deep sense of inadequacy regarding our draughtsmanship. The staff were fairly curt, but I suppose they had to put up with engineers wanting plans printed instantly, or looking for plans with inadequate information. That was not including a number of jokes played on new entrants, like being sent for a long wait (paperweight), and getting one! Eventually one was accepted.

A small subsection that we occasionally used was the Tracing Bureau, a group of girls who traced the plans on to drawing linen. Girls were a rarity, and it seemed that it had been the policy of the LMSR to engage the services of ladies in their fifties with grey hair and ginger moustaches as secretaries. That observation landed me in trouble more than once. The work of the Tracing Bureau was immaculate

and usually flawless. The Bureau was supervised by 'Tink', a glamorous lady probably in her early 40s, a somewhat daunting prospect to a teenage youth. A visit to the Bureau was much sought after by the younger men, but Tink knew all about men who were spending far too long with one of her girls, and could administer a sharp dismissal when required. A few years later I worked in the Surveyors' section, which was adjacent, and it was amusing to see her at work. I am sure she used an egg timer!

Most of my involvement early in my career was with bridge work, mainly reconstruction but sometimes major repairs. The work was simple draughtsmanship under instruction, together with the teaching at college and from seniors in the office. The plans were either for reinforced concrete (RC) slabs or steelwork detailing. Site erection or repairs still made use of site riveting, which was on its way out, replaced by fitted bolting a few years later, then by high strength bolting. Welding was beginning to appear, replacing the massive and very heavy riveted plate girders of the past at the reconstruction stage. Site riveting seems positively prehistoric from today's perspective. A site forge was set up trackside and used to heat the rivets to bright red heat, and when the steel components were

offered up and held temporarily, the rivets were thrown up to the riveter by dextrous use of shovels and tin cans, caught and placed with tongs. Leather gloves were essential! One man held a dolly behind the rivet while another hammered the head with a power riveter. For obvious reasons the strength of site riveting was taken as half that of shop fitted riveting.

Underbridge renewals were normally in RC, which I began to realise, was a massive and inefficient design compared with the new prestressed concrete (PC) system, about which I began to learn at college. This can be seen by comparing the original bridges on the M1 with later ones elsewhere on motorways. Interestingly, while searching for plans, I found a display showing the underbridges renewed on the Scottish Region in 1948 as a result of flooding between Grantshouse and Berwick. They were all to the LMR RC standard design, with the distinctive if somewhat over-the-top square section RC handrails. Almost certainly the designs were prepared at Euston and the RC units produced at Newton Heath Concrete Depot.

Reinforced concrete (RC) was a method of bridge design in which the bridge comprised a series of concrete beams rectangular in section, say 3ft wide and 20ft long. Concrete can withstand enormous compression stresses but has little tensile strength. When a beam is under load, the upper half is in compression and the lower in tension. In RC the tensile stresses are taken by steel reinforcement instead. In practice, RC work carries extra steel in order to distribute stresses from uneven curing and setting, and from applied loads.

Prestressed concrete (PC) differs in that the beam section as mentioned above, is lighter. A series of tendons, bars, or single wires are located accurately in the formwork so as to induce stresses of opposite polarity to those imposed under load. There are several systems, one using single wires which have a tensile load applied before the concrete is poured, and the wires are only cropped when at least 75-80% concrete strength is attained. Concrete sleepers, smaller beams, and building items such as lintels are manufactured in this way. For larger beams, ducts are cast into the concrete which are level for prestressing bars, or parabolic in the case of tendons. A tendon is a group of wires, say 6-10 loosely wired together for handling purposes. On attaining sufficient strength, the formwork is removed and the prestressing bars or tendons are stressed.

Calculating the stresses through manufacture up to the completion of the bridge is much more complex. The stresses initially must not exceed maximum compression value, nor incur other than small tension values. As the beam reaches its maximum strength there is a slight loss of stress which has to be anticipated. Then there is crane handling and snatch loading as slings tighten. Beams have to be supported at the ends only, as their design requires. If mishandled the beam can self-destruct somewhat explosively, and there were some cautionary tales early in their development. The advantage of PC is a weight saving of about a third, which offers the opportunity to build longer clear spans and far more elegant and economical structures.

When I went out, at first it was with a senior engineer, learning, assisting inspection, measuring up, drawing up plans for the senior man, and later taking a larger responsibility for design. Site visits were usually to the Birmingham or Manchester areas, or less commonly beyond Preston. Having left the main line, the bridge or site of work was reached using the local services. Having stepped off the main line train, one was dependent upon the infrequent services of secondary routes with Fowler 2-6-4Ts, the last few Midland Compounds and 2P 4-4-0s, and the newer Ivatt 2-6-0s and 2-6-2Ts. In those days the railway had very few departmental road vehicles, and staff were expected to make their way about by train. It is worth reminding readers that down country public road transport was scarce almost to the point of non-existence. Worse still, one was dependent all too often on anecdotal evidence rather than a published bus service timetable. Life then involved a lot of waiting.

The work of those early site visits left me with a vivid impression of the state of some LMR bridges, many suffering a serious lack of maintenance that could not be blamed entirely on the Second World War. We owe an immeasurable debt to the foresight of Victorian engineers, who built to last. In the 1950s there were still areas of the LM Region affected by coal mining, and salt extraction in Cheshire, occasionally affecting the integrity of the substructure – the footings, abutments and wingwalls. Obviously routes had been prioritised so that those on the main lines were in reasonable condition, but on low speed freight-only routes in the coalfields there were some structures in a poor state; safe, but expensive to maintain. A Mining Engineer resided at Derby, dealing with relations with the National Coal Board. Subsidence due to salt extraction made surveying difficult, and affected both bridges and track levels. To avoid continuing problems of subsidence after electrification, Elton Viaduct, between Crewe and Sandbach, was renewed by using a cell structure built from RC pipes. It allowed the stream to flow as before, and the track levels above could be restored by interposing another row of RC pipes.

One of the first bridges that I assisted a senior engineer in examining was North London Line No.116, over Caledonian Road. I was told to take a chipping hammer and check the webs of each box girder for rust, especially at the ballast level. I was astonished when, at the first stroke, the head of the hammer went straight through the web! Most bridges were off the main line, and the superstructures were often in a poor state. The LMR identified bridges by numbers, and the lines were referred to by their original names, such as

High in the Pennines on the Settle-Carlisle line, No.44828 heads a southbound freight through Dent on 25 March 1964.

One of the grand old ex-MR 3Fs and another common sight in the early days, No.43586 at Manningham shed on 21 July 1962. An MR man once assured me that you only had to show a 3F the firing shovel for it to steam.

Bridge 66 on the Eccles, Tyldesley and Wigan line, for which I did a minor plan detailing steelwork. Travelling to remote locations such as bridges on the Skipton & Morecambe line or Cockermouth, Keswick & Penrith took ages. One of my early jobs was a pair of farm bridges, 92 and 93 on the Skipton & Morecambe line. They were renewed in timber, which was certainly a design experience. Timber had not been used in bridgeworks for years, and it was only after much searching around that I found the permissible design stresses and design loading.

Students were expected to spend time visiting interesting civil engineering works, not just on the railway. Fairly early in my career a number of us were advised that a bridge erection was programmed soon, and we might find it interesting. Attendance was virtually compulsory. It was one of the first PC overbridges. It was the renewal of the bridge carrying King Henry's Walk over the North London line, between Canonbury and Dalston, a clear four track span. The bridge, as far as I recall, had a skew about 30° from square, requiring the beams to be erected in echelon by two road cranes positioned on each abutment. On site, everyone was there, the then CCE J. Taylor Thompson and his assistant CCE A.N. Butland, and most of the senior men from the Bridge Office. As the beams were lifted up off the train and swung

into position, everything went smoothly, but with about two thirds of the deck in position, it was clear that something was wrong. Some men, blissfully unaware of the H&S Act yet to come, had clambered on to the newly erected beams and checked that the ducts for the transverse prestressing lined up. They didn't.

Unless individual beams were somehow linked to act together, their differential deflections under load would make them act like piano keys, destroying the waterproofing and the road surface above. RC beams and slabs had a layer of structural concrete above to achieve this, making them even heavier and less economical. The PC beams here were rectangular in section, and were linked by transverse prestressing with rods or cables, holding the whole deck tightly together as one structural member. To align King Henry's beams for transverse prestressing, some would have failed to land on the abutments. The ducts were badly out of alignment, and it was decided to complete the deck so as to release the train and cranes, and reopen the line. When the last beam swung into place, a recently erected pilaster (The plinth at each end of the parapet) was sent flying. It was not a good day, and one felt for the Resident Engineer (RE). I would guess that the placing of the transverse ducts failed to allow for the skew, but quite what was done to

complete the bridge I cannot recall. Later I was attached to a group that walked most of the Euston-Crewe main line, surveying overbridges and other obstacles prior to electrification. There was a lot of walking to be done to cover the many routes, particularly in the Birmingham area. Pairs of engineers walked over sections of the line, noting and surveying all structures on the way that would need to be rebuilt, lifted or removed. This was useful to me in getting route knowledge not only of structures, but the geography, the services over them and how they were worked. The main line passenger services were hauled by rebuilt Scots, Patriots and Jubilees almost overwhelmingly, with the Pacifics on the Anglo-Scottish services and some of the Liverpool and Cumbrian services. The slower passenger services were worked sometimes by older locos or varieties of 2-6-4T, and usually the inevitable Black Five, 8F or an 0-6-0 worked the freight services.

As one of that team, apart from getting plenty of exercise, I learnt a great deal about the main line and its infrastructure. There were many more arch bridges on the line, and these needed to be profiled and related to track levels. Some were circular and some elliptical arches, and one, between Wolverhampton and Stafford was parabolic, most unusually. A number were farm bridges, where severance had

Above. The rebuilt Stafford station in 1962, a glimpse of the style and appearance of future replacements for the smoke blackened rusting and neglected stations of the post-war period.

Left. The renewal of the underbridge cross girders near Wolverton, using the 75t breakdown crane, in 1961. We were beginning to get 9Fs instead of 8Fs on engineering trains.

An overbridge carrying a country lane is being rebuilt here in 1961, in order to provide clearances for 25Kv. The space between each wrought iron girder was filled with an arch, sprung from the bottom flanges of the main girders, called a 'Jack Arch'. The spring course can be seen on the nearest girder.

removed the raison d'être, and these were demolished later. Off the main line there were a number of routes surveyed, mainly around Birmingham, some of which are in use with electric traction, and some of which are now under housing estates. At Hammerwich we had to survey a rather badly leaking aqueduct, for which the clearances were quite tight for steam traction. For electrification they were impossible. In passing, one of the more sophisticated office jokes was to get a junior to design a replacement aqueduct, allowing for the live load of a barge passing over.

Most of the arch bridges had to be rebuilt to achieve electrification clearances. Early on, I think after some trial work on the Crewe-Manchester route, the CCE decided against track lowering. Track drainage – if it existed – would not prevent flooding in wet weather, and the provision of adequate drainage would have been enormously expensive, even more so than the provision of overhead clearances. And of course to function properly, a drainage scheme needs an outlet, which on level track can be something of a problem. It was a good decision.

Often we had to thumb a lift on a passing freight or light engine to reach the location where work finished the day before. Looking back, it was a blessing that freight usually moved at about 20-30mph, and one could get around in this way. Care was needed, especially with faster freights, since they didn't

necessarily stop in a convenient station area. As implied earlier, road transport paralleling the Trent Valley route was scarce, although rural bus services long since forgotten were still in operation. Working down the main line north of Rugby, the variety of bridges (over and under), types of permanent way and the passing traffic were all interesting. One surprise to me was the unexpected discovery of the NCB Beyer-Garratt working at Baddesley Colliery in the sidings.

There was a fascinating intersection bridge north of Nuneaton, known as Fielding's Folly. It consisted of a pair of continuous girders spanning the four tracks on a skew, constructed as traditional plate girders, but with the web depth varied quite considerably to provide the necessary strength to resist the shear and bending stresses. The construction and erection of this pair of huge girders must have been a major task. The purpose of a continuous girder is to use the bending stresses over one span to reduce those in the adjacent spans. However, the saving in structural steelwork tended to be outweighed by the enormous complication of construction and the necessary structural strength to ensure that the built-up assembly acted as a truly single and continuous unit. It was a design technique rarely used in my experience. It certainly couldn't have helped that the bridge was on a considerable skew, needing heavy bracing to carry the

torsional stresses under load. Fielding was, I believe, the Bridge Engineer at one time, and this was his 'Great Bear'. I daresay he was roundly cursed by those who had to build it. The line was closed and the bridge scrapped in the early 1960s.

Many of the overbridges were clear four track spans, and frequently we ran into trouble, allowing the steel tape to sag on to the tracks, with disastrous results. Some minutes later one of the big 4-6-0s would appear, labouring up to speed, with the crew making a series of gestures that left little to the imagination! One particular section springs to mind, from Colwich to Stafford. Beyond the bridge over the Trent, the line passed through the Anson Estate, in the middle of which was Shugborough Tunnel (770 yards). There was an unusual ornamental underbridge over a drive on the estate leading to Shugborough Hall, and a cast iron aqueduct by the tunnel portal carrying a small trout stream. At the time it was almost dry. Curiously, the latter had an overflow chute on to the track, which seemed a strange arrangement, almost certainly unique, that probably emanated from the original sale agreement for the Trent Valley line. The advice of the ganger was against walking through the tunnel: it was curved and constantly filled with smoke, and someone had been 'knocked down' recently – a euphemism.

So the four of us set off, climbing

the very steep bank to the top of the hill, which was no easy task with the cumbersome surveying instruments of the day. At the top there was a large folly – a Hadrian's Arch – standing in an overgrown field. Then we slid down the equally steep face to the north tunnel portal, an ornamental structure known as 'The Gates of Jerusalem'. We finished at the closed station of Milford & Brocton, surveying the metal bridge over the main line. In order to return to Stafford, four of us got a lift on a pickup goods from the down yard, hauled by a Super D 0-8-0, two with the guard and two of us on the loco. The driver and the guard were at odds since the latter had failed several times to check that all the wagons to be picked up were coupled, needing him to set back repeatedly. When the outlet signal on to the down slow came off, it appeared to be time for the driver to settle accounts, for he swung the regulator fairly wide open, paused, shut it and then cracked it open. The Super D flung itself forward, the couplings tautened as the slack was taken up, and my colleagues on the guard's brake experienced the phenomenon of infinite acceleration!

With colleague David, on the sandwich course referred to earlier, I spent three winters studying under some very excellent lecturers. Life was very much like any college campus, working hard and doing the sort of mad things that the young did, rag days, inter-college rivalry, a sort of wine, women and song existence. In particular the greater understanding of structural design principles brought a greater

confidence back at the office, and I found that analysis from first principles was a more certain approach, if slower than using the office charts.

We had the feeling that, as the first two students, the administration had not really caught up with us, as after the first winter we were sent to the Survey Section, which was not on the normal round of experience for students and graduates. It was, however, an interesting and useful spell, complementing college studies, and giving greater confidence in using what were in those days quite delicate instruments. One of the first was a survey on the little-used line from Colwich to Stoke for a new underbridge. In those days it was necessary to have a chainman to assist in taking levels or working with the theodolite. Chainmen were light duty men from p.way gangs, and were far from understanding the needs of surveying, or in some cases not much else! It was necessary to go through the plan of work carefully with them to avoid rushing to and fro all day. They helped with carrying the heavy surveying equipment of those days. It was important to book the information promptly and clearly, so that back in the office, the survey could be plotted and details added. If the details were confused, or not tied in by dimensions, it was a bit too late! One of the first surveys, when plotted, showed the level of a stream to be a couple of feet above the surrounding field, which was certainly novel! The chainman was in the habit of collapsing the middle section of the 14ft telescopic levelling staff, the

effect of which was to make the upper readings appear 4ft 6ins higher than they really were. Experience taught me that no amount of growling at the chainman had any effect, and one simply had to be vigilant.

Other surveys were at Stoke-on-Trent, Northwich, Bletchley and Rugby. Two interesting surveys which were in fact a waste of time were at Claydon Jct and Euxton Jct. It was proposed to construct a new spur off the GC near Calvert, to serve the proposed new yard at Swanbourne, near Bletchley, so that southbound freight off the GC could reach the new yard via Claydon. Fortunately Gerry Fiennes at the BRB put paid to both proposals when at the BTC. Unfortunately he was too late for the Bletchley Flyover. I was glad that a senior colleague, Peter Smith, dealt with the survey for Swanbourne. The local landowner was fiercely opposed to any flyover taking his land, and instructed his gamekeeper suitably. Confronted with a 12 bore, Peter retreated leaving matters to the legal department! The small survey at Bletchley was part of the planning for the flyover, but so many passers-by questioned us that I passed it off as a new road system, which no doubt set the cat among the pigeons!

The survey at Euxton Jct was for a new flyover for the down services from Manchester to Preston. We worked with a senior surveyor, named, I believe, Charles Haunton, who was good company. The reason for my uncertainty is that he was universally known as Haunty by everyone in the office. His main attribute was a habit of bursting

'Super D' No.49430 shunts near Wednesfield. In my early days the 0-8-0s were fairly commonplace and despite their antique appearance, they were hardworking and capable. Perhaps not so good as the 8Fs that gradually displaced them, but certainly good enough most of the time.

The last days of Bletchley shed. Class 5s Nos.45292 and 45337 wait at the north end on 26 January 1964.

There were few 'Super Ds' left in service by 1964-65, and to track one down it was necessary to travel to Bushbury, where 48895 was working a freight near Wednesfield.

into great gusts of laughter, even for example when the steward serving coffee was thrown off balance as we bounced through Nuneaton, pouring coffee and milk over the table, and me! The poor man, expecting an angry reaction, was baffled at Haunty's hysterics.

The survey was quite extensive, but it came to nothing eventually. There was quite a lot of traffic moving on the junction, and life was made more interesting with periodic explosions from the munitions factory at nearby Chorley. Both Royal Scots passed here very often, and one day when I was taking measurements in the middle of the S&C, I could hear the SR diesels 10201 and 10202 approaching with the up train, and I could see CITY OF BRADFORD approaching on the down at speed. I knew that it was not a good idea to stand too near because of falling coal, and so shrank behind a signal post, feet from the down fast. Watching 46236 swaying and speeding towards me, I can assure you Dear Reader, that 'Big 'Un' sounded very much an understatement!

It was a tradition of those days that each office in the CCE's Dept saved scrap

drawings, and made a display at each Christmas. There was of course a great deal of waste paper from the Print Room as well. I remember the 1953 display, which was a huge pantomime stage, with photographs of prominent characters in the office on the principal characters. In 1957 David and I decorated the Leading Surveyor's office as a pub, which was easy considering the number of empties available. He was impressed, but we were unaware that he was looking for two unfortunates for a job over the New Year in the frozen north. Therefore as a 'reward', David and I were sent to Horton-in-Ribblesdale at New Year to assist a senior surveyor, Carl Potts, to survey the connections to the Settle Lime Sidings. This was before global warming had been discovered, and as we made our way north behind a Jubilee, piloted by a 2P 4-4-0, it grew colder and colder. I remember feeling sorry for the crew of the 2P, with an open cab – maybe not so open as a GNR one – being propelled along at 80mph plus, the temperature but a degree or two above freezing. I doubt the poor old 2Ps had been pushed along at such speeds before.

We were encumbered with 1940-50

vintage surveying instruments with heavy hardwood tripods. Former employees of Ordnance Survey adopted a very casual approach to travel and overnight lodging, and we had reached Settle before finding accommodation at Horton. After considerable conflicting evidence from a few local people, it was a great relief to see the ancient bus arrive at Settle in heavy falling snow, bound for Hawes. I recall vividly the rattling and bumping bus on which we reached Horton from Settle on a freezing cold evening. As we pottered slowly up Ribblesdale, the night sky cleared revealing a magic scene in the moonlight, freezing hard. A down freight kept pace with us, the light from the firehole door reflected in the trail of exhaust, one of those dramatic pictures that remains in the mind over the years.

The Settle-Carlisle was a very different railway. It was utterly freezing cold, but the occasional burst of sunlight revealed a breathtaking landscape, and one could understand the attraction of the railway to many people, although it looked as though life was hard in the upper dales. Walking around on track was very slippery, especially the sleepers. The down expresses were moving quite

Viaducts were not often a cause for concern, except that if there was a problem, it would be a big one! Here at Lambrigg, the spandrels have shown a tendency to bulge, hence the use of tiebars and plates above the arch ring. A fine structure which the designer would have been proud of.

Four views of a typical small bridge renewal. No.11 needed heavy repairs to the abutment and the wrought ironwork was heavily corroded. It had clearly not been maintained or painted for decades, and the design allowed pockets of rainwater to corrode the girders at node points in their construction. These two shots show the Up goods span No.2.

In these two views in 1963 the Down goods and Down goods loop span is shown both above and below. The poor condition can be seen in the upper shot. The abutment has been stabilised with mass concrete.

A pile test, actually at Euston in this case. The test pile had two others bored nearby, but not too close to disturb the ground. Then a 'kentledge beam' was erected above so that it was held down by the adjacent piles. Once the concrete had developed its full strength, a load was gradually applied to the test pile and any movement noted. In this case there was no movement.

It was less common to build new bridges beneath the railway. Some idea of the extent of the temporary works can be gained from this picture, taken at Bletchley. A Temporary Speed Restriction (TSR) was applied to all lines above, usually 20mph as they were carried on temporary waybeams.

Something of a contrast... The great bridge over the Forth, showing the rake of the cantilevers rising from a wider base. This is to counteract the considerable wind loading arising from the size of the bridge and its exposed location. In any selection of great railway bridges the Forth Bridge must be one of the top three or four.

Above. The Forth Road Bridge under construction with the main cables being 'spun'. Each cable comprised 11,600 individual tendons (as I recall) which had to be paid out over the river. The work at this stage comprised paying-out tendons of high strength steel in pairs, over the Forth. It was complicated by the range of expansion between midday and midnight which could be as great as two metres. With spans of this length the curvature of the earth became a significant factor.

Bottom left. The long approach viaducts of the Forth railway Bridge. To the right can be seen the Queens Ferry.

Left. The Road Bridge anchorage showing the tendons splayed out from the main cable.

Above. The 'Cathedral of Steel' in June 1962.

The technique of building bridges and sliding them into position has become more common over the decades. Here a slab is being rolled in on a load-bearing track. This view shows the transverse pre-stressing, successfully achieved in this case.

The intersection bridges south of Rugby, where the down Northampton lines cross the WCML. The down and down goods pass under the left-hand span, and the up line is on the right-hand side. One can see from the construction of the main girders, necessarily long due to the extreme skew, that examination and repair would be protracted and difficult. This area was on soft clay, and the vibrations set up by passing trains, especially freight, could be felt well away from the tracks.

Etherow Viaduct on the Glossop branch, is an example of a major structure that needed strengthening. Intermediate piers were built, one in the river below. The resulting appearance is, structurally, a muddle.

slowly, and freights even slower, but one had to remember that Horton-in-Ribblesdale was on a long bank at 1 in 100, to which we had no equivalent in the south. Contrariwise, one had to watch carefully for up services, running quite quickly and silently, the sound masked by the fallen snow. This was a real danger. Holbeck's Scots were rarely seen in London, and on the down run some were piloted by Black Fives. On New Year's Eve we started work, and it was so cold that I remember my fingers sticking to the theodolite. Resort had to be made frequently to the warmth of the signalbox. In the evening we all went to a ceilidh at Hawes. The cold had given way to torrential rain, but in the journey across Blea Moor heavy rain gave way to heavy snow. Two hours into the New Year we found ourselves helping push the coach through a drift on the way back to Horton! Later that day the railway was covered in deep snow, which silenced approaching trains even more, and made walking even more hazardous with snow covering the S&T dept wires and rodding. The survey was fairly straightforward. There was no traffic from the sidings, being New Year, and MARGARET, the company's 0-6-0ST was out of steam in her shed.

One of the more interesting tasks arose from the proposed alterations at

Crewe Works for building and repairing diesel and electric traction. The Works was another world. Entry and exit was through a gatehouse, and passes were demanded. The two of us were not quite searched, but closely scrutinised both entering and leaving each time presumably to ensure that we were not making off with a piston rod or chimney. Inside, we were treated like aliens, stared at and regarded with curiosity. Almost every time I paused to watch something interesting, sooner or later a blue coated foreman figure would challenge me. I remember watching an 8F being wheeled when the man in charge told me to go away as I was not allowed to watch. He got a dusty answer, but looking back I wonder whether he thought that I was doing a time and motion study. This was being introduced in various departments and was not well received by the trade unions in particular. If I was asked to take somebody's photograph with the Dumpy level once, it was a hundred times. There were compensations, however, such as the sight of freshly repaired and painted locomotives. A few ancient 0-6-0 tanks wheezed around with wagons of this and that, and motored trolleys carted heavy components from shop to shop. I remember such fine sights as DUCHESS OF ABERCORN standing in

the sunshine, gleaming with fresh paint. 9F 2-10-0s were still under construction, and one or twice a gleaming new one appeared from the Paint Shop.

It was difficult to concentrate on the surveying work when there were so many fascinating things to see, for example watching a skilled painter hand lining a Black Five cab side and tender. I gained the impression that Crewe dealt with repairs fairly slickly, but possibly more locos underwent intermediate repair rather than a full general repair. Locos were broken down into components for attention in the main works or one of the other shops very quickly. The noises emanating from the Boiler Shop at times would have wakened the dead! One of the problems in surveying here was the number of wagons or dead locos on roads in the survey, although one road turned out to have only three locos – withdrawn Beyer Garratts. From time to time the good offices of the shunter were necessary to clear various gaps for measuring survey lines. Taking levels in order to plot the topography was difficult due to the large number of obstacles, but it was solved in an unique way. With the aid of a borrowed ladder, the dumpy level was set up on top of the Belpaire firebox of a spare Pacific boiler, from where most of the obstructed area could be seen. After all, the boiler was stood like others, on sleepers, and was unlikely to move at all.

After the line by line surveys referred to earlier, more detailed surveys of special structures followed, such as the flyovers south of Rugby. The volume of work was such that some of us were moved from wasting time in the New Works Office (which had nothing that we birds of passage could be used on) to helping out in the Electrification Office. Work here involved smoothing the long sections, and designing bridge reconstructions. The long sections were detailed gradient diagrams, and it was necessary to have a smoother profile for 100mph running. Having then established the future rail levels at each overbridge, the electrification clearance would then determine the soffit (underside of the bridge deck) level. New bridges were higher: track lowering, as mentioned, had been ruled out by the CCE since it would undermine the bridge footings and cause drainage problems. Raising bridges brought its own problems, such as raising road levels. Intersection bridges were more difficult, since lifting the bridge would raise the rail tracks above, and it was not easy to run out an increase in height. If there was any adjacent S&C, the problem got rapidly worse.

Several of the younger men were now able to design PC structures, which were considerably more slender than RC. We were in an unusual position, for the senior men were trained in RC

and had only a sketchy understanding of PC. With all due respect, a few of the old boys' understanding of first principles of RC was rather shaky. What made it more difficult for them was that they used graphs to establish RC structural data rather than work from first principles, whereas for PC one had to work from first principles. On replacement road bridges we used a higher slenderness ratio, from memory 40% greater, and reduced the depth of the beams at each end where necessary to ease the lift in the road surface. The apparent flexibility of the beams was reduced by stressing them transversely, so as to act as a homogeneous slab. This was the intention years before at King Henry's Walk.

The resulting designs had to be translated into working drawings, and there were amusing sounds of bafflement, doubt and disapproval from our seniors. Charlie Kerslake, one of the senior engineers, responded to the cutting edge of PC design by muttering 'Ooh crikey!', rubbing his head furiously and pacing up and down, much to our amusement. Some overbridges had replaced level crossings over the years, and the approaches were quite steep. The counties had set a maximum inclination on bridge approaches at 1 in 19, although a number were steeper *before* reconstruction. The new bridge lifted the road surface, and in some cases the lift had to be run out over some distance, including side roads. If there were shops or houses on the

approaches, the whole rebuilding project became much more complicated due to the need to control and direct rainfall run-off.

Intersection bridges were fairly uncommon, but when it was necessary to achieve electrification clearances for the lower tracks, design was much more difficult as I've said. They were usually metal bridges, and it was not easy to reduce the constructional depth since the designs were usually quite economical. Substitution of a PC bridge deck actually increased the depth. To raise the tracks overhead, the lift had to be run out over a considerable distance, although one could shorten that distance for low speed goods lines. Bridge No.100 at Edge Hill was the most difficult I encountered, due to the proximity of S&C connections. The main line dropped down past Edge Hill depot, while tracks turned off on the down side, rose and swung across the main line en route for Wavertree Goods, the docks, etc. It was difficult to do more than shave off a few inches with the new design, and the rest of the increase in headroom had to be achieved by track lifting. The detailed design was developed later, by which time a significant amount of freight infrastructure was redundant. This interesting work was cut short by National Service.

In 1963 I returned to the Bridge Office to carry out two designs for professional qualification, one an overbridge, the other an underbridge. Two developments had taken place by then,

Black Five No.45434 ambles along the once-beautiful Lune Valley with a down freight, near Dillicar, 23 March 1964.

A typical lunchtime view with two named trains. Both trains were doubleheaded with Class 5s. In platform 1, 45257 has piloted No.46245 CITY OF LONDON, while in platform 2, No.45376 has piloted an unidentified sister 4-6-0.

A Pacific had departed Camden, clearly intended for the 10.40am Perth departure. My wait, on a bright but freezing morning, was well worthwhile, as No.46234 DUCHESS OF ABERCORN came roaring over the summit at Camden bank with the train, a stunning picture.

of which the first was the design of a standard type A underbridge, which eased the design and drawing production work for subsequent reconstructions. Having completed the design of the first, an underbridge using the standard type A layout, I was not surprised to hear that the Institution of Civil Engineers required something more challenging. They had had enough of candidates submitting Standard A designs, which were in fact fairly simple designs, and something more challenging was required. So it was back to the drawing board and calculation sheets. My type A design was in fact three separate spans carrying five tracks; quite complex, but it would have been pointless to argue. So a second design task was given me, also in the Nottingham area, but now an overbridge.

The second development that had taken place was a more extensive use of isotropy. In practice the imposed loads were concentrated either as rail tracks for an underbridge, or as wheel loads on an overbridge. The use of concrete beams of greater slenderness placed greater emphasis on the resulting 'piano-keyboard effect' of loaded beams tending to act independently, and the need to guard against it in the design, as mentioned earlier. Design made greater use of isotropic slabs, which

were a series of slender beams prestressed together transversely to act as a single structural member, a slab. To link beams transversely, the system needs to resist the shear forces between adjacent beams carrying different loads. Later designs effectively inserted an in situ RC beam between each precast beam as a shear connector rather than use transverse prestressing. The main problem with transverse prestressing was and is one that should be simplicity itself – getting the transverse ducts to line up so that the prestressing rods/tendons could be inserted. It was far more difficult with skew bridges like King Henry's Walk, where the transverse ducts had to be on the skew, and not at right angles to the longitudinal axis. A tendon was a group of 6-9mm high tensile cables, flexible and less easy to install but with a greater grip on the surrounding concrete arising from the greater superficial area per square inch cross section. Trying to insert a reluctant tendon 20-40ft long, flopping about on a crane, into a transverse duct a shade tight, was not fun. Skyhooks are an essential part of civil engineering plant.

The advantage of isotropic slab design was that something like a third of the design load on a single beam is transferred to the adjacent beams, and imposed loads are carried by the whole slab and not individual beams. This

approach allowed the use of thinner slabs. It was this design that I used on the overbridge. The longitudinal beams were prestressed, and as the overbridge was square, I used transverse prestressing. Although the lessons of King Henry's Walk remained in my mind, this bridge was dead square. However, I played safe with Lee McCall high tensile prestressing rods rather than tendons which were now more widely used. As the deck was to be erected in two halves, I halved rod length, allowing a temporary transverse prestress to be applied to the first half of the deck. When the full deck had been erected, both sets of half rods were joined with threaded couplers and fully stressed. This time the Institution was happy with the design and it was submitted for the professional interview.

Years later I attempted to find the two bridges as a matter of curiosity, but both had disappeared. I started to feel old.

Euston could certainly be relied on for the splendid sight of a Stanier Pacific, posed at the stops on platforms 1 or 2. No.46238 CITY OF CARLISLE again is at old platform 1 with the Ulster Express (headboard removed), a tracery of the old roof as a background.

An unidentified Black Five heads towards Skipton with a service from Carlisle in 1961.

A 4F 0-6-0 brings a special service into Skipton in 1961.

Longsight Electric Traction Depot in 1961, with a row of gleaming new 25Kv AC locos, and an EMU behind.

Truly an age apart, No.48895 still shunting (see page 16) at Wednesfield in 1963.

Although a poor quality print, it is a rare opportunity to see one of the Southern diesels, 10201, pull into Rugby Midland with the 14.30 Birmingham 'Two Hour' service.

0-8-0 No.49430 pulls away with a local freight.

A view from Rugby Flyover with an EE Type 4 on an express, on the up fast.

Chapter Two: The District - On Track

Having passed all my exams successfully, my reward was a letter from a Miss Evans somewhere in the ether telling me to report for National Service at 16TRRE at Malvern. This was an introduction to a largely wasted two years with National Service at the Longmoor Military Railway. National servicemen were by that time barred from anything of interest, and being a railway engineer, unusually for the army, I found myself at Longmoor. It was a curious place as one might expect from a juxtaposition of the remnants of the 1939-45 war with a railway. The railway was a poor outfit, the army poorer. I asked a friend, Capt Walton, that if this was the victorious army, how on earth did the Germans lose? His tart reply was that the *real* army went home by 1947, and he had to cope with a lot of rubbish that remained behind. That was my impression but I chose not to say so!

The railway was a poor old thing, but I applied for a cab pass, and rode on the 0-6-0T, 2-8-0 and 2-10-0 locos there. One of the two 2-10-0s on two carriages could achieve an astonishing rate of acceleration! The line traversed mainly heath country, and it was very easy to start lineside fires with too exuberant use of full regulator! One had a leaky regulator, with the result that a full brake application failed to stop the train at Weaversdown platform. Looking back I had one door left on the platform, from which an RSM descended and walked away. Next time remember to slam the regulator hard shut! The 0-6-0Ts were a rough lot, and the old saying about skins off rice puddings applied.

When I had returned from National Service, the CCE's office had acquired a senior engineer responsible for student and graduate training, W.H. (Bill) Best, formerly District Engineer at Lancaster, and rumoured to be related to the late Lord Stamp. Bill was fairly laid back, but was a very helpful chap indeed. With his agreement I had spells on the District and on site in order to gain my professional qualification as a chartered civil engineer.

I returned to civilisation in September 1960 to start at London District, the offices of which were at St.Pancras station. The railway had moved on in two years. The District embraced the main line from Euston to Stoke Hammond, south of Bletchley, from St.Pancras to Oakley, north of Bedford, parts of the old GCR not maintained by London Transport, and the secondary lines within that area. The District Engineer (DE), Freddie Fawcett (FF) had a drawing office split into permanent way and works (bridges and structures) together with clerical support and the inevitable staff section. Actually I found the district staff very different from head office, helpful and friendly, and vital to the smooth running of the office.

I was placed on the p. way side of the office, dealing with track relaying, reballasting and formation work. Within days I went out on the Midland main line, and it was immediately obvious that this was a different world, a long way from stresses, deflections, steel and concrete. *This* was the part of the railway infrastructure that earnt the money, and while bridge design included factors of safety, one only had to see a Jubilee racing round the curve at St Albans to appreciate that Safety of the Line was a much closer concern to everyone. Standing alongside, one could appreciate the amount of vibration and vertical movement of the track very fully.

The office was off the old hotel entrance, with huge windows, high ceilings and plenty of space. The DE and his assistants were on the first floor, reached up the grand spiral staircase and along high and wide corridors, 'murmurous with BR Persian carpet', as *The Times* described it. It was, in a way, a wonderful office, and felt good. Rather like an elderly aunt, it had the personality of one who had known better and more gracious days, but had fallen on more testing times. It epitomised the faded glory of the old Midland Hotel that it once was, with

The typical ballast train of the early 1960s, an 8F with 16 ton mineral wagons, approaching Roade cutting from Northampton in 1961.

Relaying at St.Albans North in 1961. Despite the appearance of chaos, the new 'S&C' (Switches and Crossings) was built up on the adjacent headshunt. The layout was then dismantled into large sections which were then slid across using old bullhead rail laid flat. In 1961, we had only brute manpower, and Sub-Inspector Joe Bass has to control the movement safely with a large gang of men.

The loose-heel switch was a staple of the pre-nationalisation railway, away from the fast lines. The fishplate on the right had the two fishbolts of the short switch rail left slightly loose to allow the switch rail to move clear of wheel flanges.

Railjoints were unsupported on UK railways, but there were occasional experiments with supported fishplates. The Caledonian Railway once used a joint supported fishplate but it was discontinued.

As lengths of CWR (Continuous Welded Rail) were laid, the adjacent jointed track was protected from expansion of the CWR by 'breather' switches, which absorbed the expansion. As CWR became more common, the breathers were removed. A problem associated with them was that they were slightly more prone to cracking.

In the late 1950s track relaying used 60ft panels. A wood sleepered panel weighed about 4-4½ tons, well within the capacity of a TRM (Track Relaying Machine). The change to concrete sleepers increased the weight of a 60ft panel to about 19 tons, which led to a redesign of the TRMs. Here, near Weedon in 1961, a three jib TRM is laying concrete panels, with a 350HP diesel shunter providing the motive power.

Accommodating insulated joints, required for signalling purposes, in CWR was a problem, and a number of different designs were used before the factory-assembled six-hole plate provided a satisfactory solution. This was an early design.

The TRM has lifted a panel of old track and placed it on the bogie wagons ahead, and is moving back to the other half of the train with the new concrete panels in order to pick up the next concrete panel.

A bulldozer at work, clearing an embankment slip. Slips were almost always caused by rainwater lubricating unstable slopes, and it was necessary to put in deep rubble drains – counterforts – to drain the slope and provide weight and stability. Slag blocks were available from the steelmaking industry, until better ore was imported, and now granite and similarly heavy stone is used.

grand doorways and doors, walls with elaborate decorations that suggested no change since 1922, and acres of deep pile carpets. Occasional attempts were made in hot weather to ventilate the office by opening the windows, releasing clouds of Midland Railway soot into the office. On the other hand it was restfully quiet, without the noise of multiple conversations and the click of high heels that make open offices more difficult to work in, pleasant but distracting!

I was immediately introduced to the mysteries of the world's largest Meccano set (Lego if you are under 50) that is permanent way in all its forms and the myriad components that comprise a track layout. Then, as well, there was the language, the jargon. In retrospect the District was a good place to learn about p.way, as it was an amalgam of the new designs, the existing and the old p.way. The P.Way Inspectors were each responsible for a section of route, and generally they were older men who harked back to the old days, with their own jargon. It was a time of great change, indeed there hadn't been a change of such proportions before. The traditional bullhead section rail (BH) which had been developed to the 95lb RBS (Revised British Section) was being replaced by flat-bottomed rail (FB) as lengths fell due for renewal. Several variations in weight had been

used but BR reduced the choice to 109lb for main routes and 98lb for secondary routes. In fact relaying on secondary routes used serviceable 109lb rails off the main line very often, and the 98lb section was dropped. The change to FB rail was not universally popular, either with the inspectors or some District Engineers.

As if that was not enough, continuously welded rail (CWR) was being installed as a priority on the main lines, introducing a more extended and complex system of relaying. The priority for the installation of CWR on the fast lines on the West Coast main line was such that the principle of premature relaying was established; i.e. relaying with CWR before the normal parameters required track renewal. The displaced jointed track components were used on relaying elsewhere. CWR comprised 109lb rail, but the situation with regard to fastenings and sleepers was still fluid. The CCE, Arthur Butland, was determined to achieve a direct fastening to concrete sleepers, and he was eventually successful. At the time concrete sleepers were used with Mills C clips, requiring a heavy baseplate and clips, but the 'BJB' was a direct screwed fastening being used in quantities. The WR developed the 'SHC' fastening which was excellent, far better than the BJB, but development of the Pandrol clip was not far off. By comparison with

earlier types, the Pandrol was ideal and trouble-free. The alternative to concrete sleepers was jarrah, an Australian hardwood with the Mills fastening. It was used over sections where the formation was shallow and could not be improved, but as the LM had prior call on the supplies of concrete, the Eastern/North Eastern Regions had recourse to jarrah for CWR, which actually produced a much better road.

S&C relaying comprised 109lb FB rail mounted on softwood timbers and fastened with T bolt and spring clips. This was an unsatisfactory design dating from Nationalisation which was difficult to maintain and, apart from having a myriad of components, unless the ballast was kept tightly packed it allowed vertical movement under traffic, leading to either cracked or broken rails. Connecting bolts loosened and the threads were hammered flat under traffic making tightening or replacement impossible. Bullhead relaying was confined to replacing parts of an existing layout, being fastened with oak or steel spring keys. Tunnels were laid with 97½lb BH, the slightly heavier section being justified by accelerated corrosion in the steam era. BH rail was used as it could be replaced quickly in the tunnels. It was simply a case of unbolting the fishplates, knocking the keys out, lifting out one rail, substituting a new rail and resecuring. In due course, after steam

How to de-track a Drott. With a skilful driver one could be positioned on the track without bothering with sleepers, ready for excavation once the old track was lifted. Again, not the best of ideas.

Machine drainage. A 10RB backacter sitting on a sleeper crib to allow a loaded wagon to be rolled past. Then the sleeper crib was extended over the adjacent track, 10RB was moved back into position to continue digging the drain in the six-foot.

A Drott traxcavator in action at St.Albans North.

St.Albans. The slow lines site is being cleared, with Drotts working away, Meanwhile a brand new diesel heads an up express slowly past.

Left. St.Albans. Moving one of the Drotts about. A sleeper was often placed either side of a rail to allow the machine's tracks to get a grip and climb over the rail.

Below. Sea defence work was fascinating so long as one remembered that the sea would probably win in the end. The objective was to put that event as far ahead as economically sensible.

The factory-assembled insulated joint was the best answer to the problem of providing insulation between track signalling sections. On non-electrified lines the Aster tuned track circuit was used, requiring no insulated joint, but on electrified lines using the running rails for earth return, a physical break was needed.

had finished, CWR was permitted in tunnels. This is a brief description of an incredibly detailed subject, which I will return to later.

It was not very long before I was out at weekends on engineering work. The work was at Hendon, piling the up side cutting slope and draining the six roads south of the station down to the site of the Welsh Harp station. The railway ran through a belt of yellow clay here as did all lines running north from London. Then all six roads were 'claydug' – in other words the formation was completely renewed. I was given the job of escorting the movement of the hired 19RB crane from the goods yard down to the site with a movements inspector directing the driver. The 19RB set off with the jib lowered to avoid canopies, power and telephone lines, and once clear of the station buildings, the movements inspector told the driver to lift his jib – a shade prematurely since the jib felled the trunk telephone line to Derby almost immediately. The slow lines were under possession, and once the cranes were in place, a materials train with the Dalmag diesel piling hammers

and a supply of sheet piles came up from Cricklewood on the down slow.

The work went well, piles at roughly 8ft 6ins centres with a sleeper wall between. The diesel hammer was very impressive, and I resolved to use nothing else in future. The drainage work was the first stage in the rehabilitation of the tracks. It involved digging a deep trench in the 'six-foot' between the tracks with a 10RB which was sitting on a sleeper crib across the two adjacent rails with an adjacent wagon for the spoil. The trench was lined with Weldmesh panels, the drain was laid and backfilled with ballast. When the spoil wagon was full, the whole lot had to be moved sideways to get another empty wagon alongside. There had to be a better way of doing this work, and fortunately the science of hydrostatic engineering came to our aid some years later.

Then the formation renewal started, using 19 or 22RB draglines and small dozers. The track was lifted out over say 10 lengths, and the spoil dug out and loaded, leaving a long trench some 3ft deep, the cross-fall angled towards

the new drains already installed. Then it was filled with about 9ins of sand, then plastic sheeting as an artificial water barrier, laid towards the drain, more sand, then some 12ins ballast. The track was relaid and fettled, and opened under a 20mph TSR. Once again, there had to be a better way to carry out this work. A blessed soul had started to improve things with the Drott, a tracked machine which combined the function of bulldozer with a loading shovel. The Drott could dig and then load the spoil into a wagon alongside. They could have been more robustly built, for they were such an advance on previous methods that they were worked hard every weekend. In a keenly competitive field, other manufacturers took up the baton. The whole job at Hendon lasted a year.

Moving trains about was a new experience, but the need for care, safety of everyone, and clear and unambiguous communications was repeatedly hammered home by senior engineers. The P W Inspector in charge directed movement using a whistle code – one blast for 'stop', two for 'move forward', and three for 'set back'.

Two views of a claydig – formation renewal at Hendon. The excavation is handled by small bulldozers, the alternative if all known Drotts were already booked out, and the loading was carried out by 22RB draglines. The dragline drivers were experts who could pick up a cigarette packet, so was the boast, but they were painfully slow. The dozers gave a clean base, but to get a crossfall the dragline had to dig deeper on one side, which was slow.

Millbrook relaying, near Bedford. A down express coasts by, headed by Royal Scot No.46109 ROYAL ENGINEER.

A ballast train, hauled by a former Crosti 2-10-0 No.92023, is being unloaded on the up slow.

A thermit weld being prepared. The mould is carefully secured around the joint, and the crucible, mounted on the vertical tube, is loaded with thermit powder. The mould is them heated by gas, the crucible is swung over the mould, and then fired. The liquid steel flows into the mould, and 15-20 minutes later has cooled sufficiently for the mould to be struck and some of the excess metal cropped. Once the weld has cooled to normal temperature, the excess is ground away and the railhead made smooth.

A down freight approaches Mill Hill behind a 9F 2-10-0 on the Down slow in 1961.

Everyone stood clear of the train and of course adjacent running lines. The noise on site could easily mask an approaching express. The engineering trains were a mixture, with the inevitable 8F, occasionally a Super D 0-8-0, or a BR 9F hauling a train of wagons of varying decrepitude. The CCE had hopper wagons for ballast, which were unloaded directly on or around the track beneath. Ballast for S&C came in better wooden bodied wagons, or the new Mermaid and Grampus steel wagons. The Mermaids were tipped to one side, being shackled to the opposite rail to prevent overturning, dropping 14 tons of stone in one place. With these wagons it was essential to complete unloading and release ALL of the shackles before attempting to move the train. Obvious, but I remember two incidents where some were missed: fortunately the driver stopped before any damage was done, sensing that something was wrong. The shackles were not much good afterwards!

On one occasion, the 8F bringing the materials train had considerable flats on some of the coupled wheels, together with some heavy blows at the front end. Standing at least three feet below, while the driver tried to get his wheezing and thumping loco past so as to be able to unload sand, I began wonder whether they would soon be joining me in the excavation. On another occasion, a driver refused to pass a stop signal despite standing several miles into the

possession, and I went down to reassure him that he could pass safely whilst at danger. His train was 39 loaded Mermaids, at least 800 tons, but fortunately his loco was a 9F, in ex-works condition. I remember he leaned forward, pulled the regulator open, and she just walked away with this heavy train.

Parts of the track had suffered from shortage of staff for decades, leading to blocked drains and fouled formations. One Sunday morning I had the task of getting out trial trenches between the old Ampthill station and the tunnel on the down fast line. A 'Between trains' possession (T2 in the 1970s Rule Book) had been agreed on the down fast from 8.00 to 16.00, together with a 20mph TSR during the work, since I would be weakening the area round the railjoints on a very fast section of track. I was given eight men and a sub-inspector, a lookout man with the gang, and a hand signalman at Ampthill station signalbox together with a pile of detonators. Fine. By about 10.00 the job of digging trenches in the muddy pudding that passed for a formation was half done, when I realised that while I could hear the occasional new DMU chugging along the slows, nothing had passed on the fast lines. There was an 8.50 from St.Pancras – wasn't there? Before long I heard a train in the distance, clearly moving fast, and I prompted the lookout to move everyone clear. A detonator exploded up at the station,

and the next moment a Royal Scot came hurtling into view, with eight men, lookout, sub-inspector and engineer scrambling up the cutting slope like startled rabbits. She shot past, brakes hard on, flames, sparks and smoke pouring from the brake blocks, and the train stopped at the far end of the tunnel. Shortly after, another Scot came crawling out of the tunnel with an up express, the driver carefully observing a non-existent TSR! The job was nearly complete by 11.00, and I was aware that the Thames-Clyde Express was due soon. The distant two-tone horn was the cue for everyone to scuttle up the cutting slope again, followed by the detonators and then a brand new D20 shot past at full speed and no attempt to slow down. So much for the TSR and drivers reading their notices.

One of the larger relaying tasks was at Millbrook, north of Ampthill Tunnel, and one could see why the patient preparation in the office, on site and at the manufacturers was necessary. As the cranes lifted each part into position in the prescribed order, the numbered timbers had to be first laid in order and to line so as to receive it on the baseplates. The whole operation went like clockwork. However, ballasting and fettling the track so that the line and level of the rails were correct and tightly ballasted was a long and tiring job. Electric hammers were being introduced on this work, but the noise level was very high. Such hammers were a major

The Up Midland Pullman speeds through Mill Hill in 1961.

No.92054 coasts downhill from Elstree in 1961 with a heavy part-fitted freight.

By 1960 many of the Royal Scots had been displaced from the WCML and a number were used on the Midland Division, which hitherto had managed with Jubilees. Here an up express, going hard, reaches the top of the climb from Radlett, hauled by No.46151 THE ROYAL HORSE GUARDSMAN.

The Thames Clyde Express hauled by Jubilee 45589 GWALIOR passes Elstree in fine style, going well.

The Midland Pullman at Elstree.

4F 0-6-0 No.44440 on the up slow approaching Elstree (slow lines) Tunnel, hauling the prototype BR 5MT No.73000 and 4MT 2-6-4T No.42057.

A southbound milk train, doubleheaded with an unidentified 5MT and Caprotti Class 5MT No.44756, passes Elstree on the up slow.

cause of industrial deafness, and we badly needed a tamper to ease this task.

An amusing incident occurred during the week. Dalston relaying gang were enjoying a spell 'in the country' manning the relaying, and 'Buster' the elderly 'tea boy' it turned out, had formerly worked as a butcher. The tea boy was almost as important in a gang as the ganger, organising food and tea, and often completing the timesheets on behalf of the ganger. On this occasion he had struck a bargain with a neighbouring farmer for the purchase of not only eggs but a few chickens as well. On a fine sunny morning he sat by the lineside and prepared the birds 'for the table'. Subsequently a driver of a down express mistook a cloud of plucked feathers for a fatality and (in signalling parlance) 'stopped the job' at Bedford. Freddie Fawcett had quite a few words to say about it, probably none of which are repeatable!

I was given the task of designing a new layout for St.Albans North slow lines, which was based on a complete realignment. Starting with the survey, a preliminary skirmish revealed that there was no avoiding a theodolite siting near the fast lines for at least a part of the work. Discussion with the signalman at the North box established a clear half-hour after the Blue Pullman had gone, so after she had passed with her famously shaking bogies, I set up. Having nearly finished, I then heard the signalman call out that there was a relief express coming, and within minutes a

Royal Scot appeared, at speed. Well, I was clear of the sleeper ends, but not by much, without a post to hide behind, and the slipstream could well blow the theodolite over. When they are that close, locos appear to be coming straight for you, and every instinct is to leg it. I should have moved anyway, since the passage of the train had shaken the instrument off level and I had to start again!

I had a lookout man from the length gang, an elderly character with a strong Hertfordshire accent, who bred dogs for a hobby. His accent reminded me of Bernard Miles, the actor. He was known as 'Harpic', I was told by the ganger. 'I know I shouldn't ask' I said, 'but why?' 'Clean round the bend' was the reply. I knew I shouldn't have asked. As I walked around after lunch, looking for Harpic, I found an old detonator. The only safe detonator is a dead one, and so, without further thought, I placed it on the railhead behind the ancient 3F shunting the yard. The crew were missing, and when they returned I was on my survey, and forgot. The consequences were obvious. There was a mighty explosion from the 3F as she moved, followed by the noise of shouted abuse between the footplate and the p.way hut!

The slow lines had a W alignment which was to be slued to a smooth curve. The existing layout included connections to the up yard, which was closed, and also to the middle siding. However the slow line was canted for

60mph as far as I can remember, which meant that use of the connections (through opposite curvature) involved considerable reverse cant. For that reason the new S&C layout was 'two-levelled', which meant that the rails and the timbers beneath were canted at different rates. The two-levelling was achieved by thickening the baseplates under the high rails. As the layout was on a curve, the angles and intervals between rails on the compound baseplates for the crossings changed, which made timbering and chairing extremely complex. The whole length of about 400 yards was reballasted on the new alignment, involving slues of up to 8ft. The sluing was accomplished by two gangs of temporary staff, and their discipline was good to watch as the tracks were heaved over. Fettling in the following week required both gangs. We had another case of failure to read the notices as the driver of a DMU came tearing through the 20 mph TSR, although as he was about to stop at the station we were lucky that it was only about 40 mph and not full speed. The weekday work was carried out by the Bedford relaying gang, formerly employees of the brick industry, many of whom were Italian. It was interesting to hear the ganger instructing his gang in Italian with a strong Bedfordshire accent!

The time spent at St.Pancras was valuable, linking the theory and design of college and head office with the working railway. There were the less

A down express, hauled by Jubilee No.45579 PUNJAB, coasts past relaying at Millbrook. The essential function of lining-up before fishplating was achieved by the humble sluing bar, seen on the left.

An up express at speed at Millbrook, hauled by Royal Scot No.46134 THE CHESHIRE REGIMENT piloted by Jubilee No.45664 NELSON.

Jubilee No.45589 GWALIOR at speed on an up express at Elstree.

intricate but essential tasks such as the ordering of replacement S&C components, dealing with derailments and the subsequent investigations, rail failures, and updating of records. Gradually one learnt the niceties of p.way – to talk the *argot* of switches, of crossing splices, the names of components and rails in S&C, types of fastenings, and so on. It was also excellent training in assessing the condition of track, which was extremely important since track renewal was a major determinant of the maintenance budget. It was a much smaller office than the CCE's office but with much more of a sense of teamwork. In those days all letters had a second copy on yellow paper which was subsequently circulated round the office. Communication! One benefit of the system was that when Freddie Fawcett wrote a letter, in his incomparable style, we all enjoyed it. He was good friends with Ken Tredinnick, DE at Stratford, and their exchanges over maintenance problems on the Tottenham & Hampstead or the North London were collectors' items.

Every now and then there was a derailment, and it was all hands to the pump, to investigate the cause and to restore the track. The latter was a simple case of assessing the usable track and ordering enough replacement material. The investigation was a mixture of the serious and the hilarious, with all departments determined that it was someone else's fault. FF caught a C&W inspector throwing a broken axlebox down the embankment on one occasion. The DE was unfortunate since the state of the track was there for all to see, and it is axiomatic that the rogue wagon will find a track fault on which to derail. The CMEE's carriage and wagon engineers regarded a vehicle condition as good so long as its chassis, load and springing were in order. However this was the static condition, and the dynamic behaviour, which was often the cause, could not be ascertained with any accuracy. Two identical vehicles, with leaf springing, could ride quite differently at speed. Then followed the joint inquiry, at which the general altercation continued, now with trade union assistance (?). As most involved freight, it wasn't too bad, but with passenger trains the HM Railway Inspectorate were involved and matters got much more serious.

We had one bad one on a Saturday afternoon, when a Type 2 diesel with a van train destroyed the up slow from Scratchwood Sidings to Mill Hill before the driver realised that part of his train was on the floor and stopped, best part of a mile. If I remember correctly, the cause was speed together with a few lightly laden box vans here and there in the train. It caused a substantial reprogramming of numerous social lives. Having measured up and ordered the replacement track, we paused for a few minutes. I was standing by Freddie Fawcett, with the District Operating Superintendent nearby, when a student remarked that the up slow was due for relaying, and wouldn't it be a good idea to relay it throughout now? FF motioned him to be quiet, and replied, loudly for the benefit of the DOS, *'We must learn not to capitalise on the misfortunes of our friends in the Operating Department!'* The DOS gave a sickly smile.

Maintenance was very important, although a senior bridge engineer once dismissed it as 'coordinate geometry and bum-kicking'. Originally ballast was hammered tight under the sleepers (beater packing) using a beater pick, a pickaxe with one tine fashioned into a hammer head. This was superseded by 'fly packing', where the ganger assessed

A heavy freight on the up slow at Millbrook hauled by 9F 2-10-0 No.92053. My boss, and good friend, Ken Botwright, surveys the site prior to the commencement of relaying.

the amount of vertical movement under traffic, and selected suitable stone to place under the sleeper. This system was formalised into measured shovel packing (MSP) in which the vertical rail movement was measured, in sixteenths of an inch. A standard canister of chippings spread under the sleeper below the rail seat was equivalent to one sixteenth of an inch, and the necessary packing, in canisters, was marked in the web of the rail. It was a relatively bespoke maintenance system, labour intensive, although fifty years later it may well sound like the age of the horse and cart. Chippings were unloaded into chipping bins at intervals along the trackside. It was a system that worked well, and the track stood for far longer than tamped track in those days. A similar system served the SNCF very well even into the era of very high speeds, the piles of chippings in the six-foot being a giveaway. Tampers were just being introduced, partly due to the search for greater productivity, and partly due to the crippling labour shortage in industrial and suburban areas. The tampers are basically mechanical beater packers, although they have been greatly refined from the late 1950s.

I was gaining an understanding of track maintenance, thanks to some friendly inspectors, but I suppose a fall

was inevitable. My first acquaintance with the DC lines out of Euston was between Watford Junction and Bushey, and I had not seen such poor track, loose keys, some chairscrews loose, and sleepers rattling under trains. Much of the DC lines was seriously under-maintained. The convention was to write in yellow wax crayon on the sleepers, which I did. Back in the office, I was sent to the P.Way Assistant, Derek Johnson, a very pleasant man. I was told that only P.Way Inspectors usually used yellow crayon, and the electric lines P.Way Inspector had complained to him. I explained the state of the track was bad, and Derek smiled. *'I think that the trains know the way to Euston anyway. Leave it with me, and don't do it again'.* I had learnt that the inspectors still wielded their historic power over engineers, but if there was a can to be carried, it was the engineer. The DE talked to his Chief P. Way Inspector on maintenance matters rather than his engineers. This had to change. Later that particular inspector fell from grace, due to a hydraulic lunch and a lady friend during working hours. The seventh commandment has been the undoing of many a railwayman over the years!

At the time Districts kept 'Age of Road' diagrams which were updated with each relaying item. Rail history needed to be recorded, so that rail

failures could be analysed and reported to the CCE office. Every so often a cracked or broken rail came into the office. I recall a bad one, where a triangular chunk of the rail end had broken off but remained held between the fishplates, where it had been hammered by passing traffic before the ganger had spotted it.

Gradually an understanding of p.way, its condition and behaviour was gained by observation and discussions with engineers and inspectors. Watching a P.Way Inspector (PWI) working with a gang, fine lining, was useful in learning to judge 'top' and 'line' (alignment). It was surprising how a misalignment of a fraction of an inch stood out. 'Top' was another matter, the level surface on which wheels ran. FB rail, far stronger than BH horizontally and vertically, gradually 'crippled' at the rail ends, paradoxically. Jointed FB track viewed through a dumpy level, or sighted along the railhead, looked terrible with the rail ends battered down 10-20mm, although it rode well enough. British track featured unsupported joints, unlike that of the SNCF for example, where joints were fully supported (see page 35). The SNCF also used longer fishplates and hardwood sleepers, which of course had a bearing on 'top', and the track looked much better. Experiments were carried out on

A fast freight passes Millbrook on the down fast hauled by an unidentified Class 5MT 4-6-0.

A down express passes work at Hendon behind Jubilee No.45571 SOUTH AFRICA.

BR but the advent of CWR and mechanised maintenance – tamping – would require regular sleeper spacing for maximum effect.

It was enormously valuable. However, after a year, I was moved to site work, a period of which was a requirement for professional qualification. Returning to St.Pancras 42 years later, to a beautifully restored station, was a strange experience. It is second to none, although I am quite sure that the international traffic should have gone to Euston. At the time the SR termini were full, and in any case hobbled by the lack of any clear route in with no flat junctions. St.Pancras was the only terminal north of the river said to have some capacity, although more capacity had to be constructed north of the original terminal. In my view it was a short term solution, and a more long term strategy was imperative. However, rightly or wrongly, as a result the magnificent terminal has been transformed into a jewel of architectural and structural excellence. The great Barlow roof is majestic, even though a garage forecourt has been stuck on the north end. My old drawing office is now a restaurant, and the grand staircase is now truly grand. The soot and dust of the Midland Railway is gone. Only the ghosts of the 1960s remain now.

Arising from my acquaintance with Bill Best, I became a member of the Civil Engineering Students' Association, which organised visits to interesting projects – of which there were many at that time. We had two lectures per annum at the Institution in Westminster by an eminent engineer, which was followed by supper at one of the railway hotels with the CCEs of the four London Regions. A privilege, but an opportunity to put one's foot in it in a big way! It was a very interesting experience, if nervy – a subject could turn into a question out of the blue, and it had to be answered without delay. Marcus George Russell Smith was the WR CCE, everything one would expect of a successor to IKB, Alfred Henry Cantrell on the SR, Alexander Key Terris for the ER and Arthur Norman Butland for the LMR. The first two were fairly quiet, but 'Sandy' Terris was a very interesting man, formerly District Engineer Glasgow North, which extended to Mallaig. I made sure of sitting alongside, since his reminiscences of the West Highland, especially in winter, were fascinating. He was justifiably proud of his track, and was encouraged that I knew the East Coast main line well. He was quite confident that his track was good enough whatever speed the operators could manage. One of his

early lengths of CWR at Egmanton had stood for about seven years without tamping, and he had threatened to discipline anyone using a tamper on it. Some years later I met the engineer responsible for the section, who confirmed that the threat had indeed been made! It confirmed my growing conviction that the better the new track is prepared and restored to full speed running, the better it will stand under traffic.

Sandy Terris asked me where I lived, since I knew his main line so well, which led to the question as to why I worked on the LMR and not the ER. Having explained why, Terris was firmly of the view that I should work for him, which was more than a little difficult for me since I was sat between Terris and my chief! Alfred Cantrell of the SR was often replaced by his assistant, Parker, but this gentleman had reached the dizzy heights of the profession despite refusing to accept that prestressed concrete was a safe and sound building system! I must admit to having made some contentious remarks deliberately about using PC instead of steel (which had to be painted periodically) in order to get him going!

No longer a stranger at Marylebone, the LMS having taken over; Jubilee No.45595 SOUTHERN RHODESIA, just out of works waits outside the terminus in 1963.

Chapter Three: On Site
The Up Empty Carriage Line Tunnel Widening, Temporary Parcels Depot, and Euston Reconstruction

The first project was the widening of the Up Empty Carriage Line tunnel which left the up slow at Primrose Hill just east of the slow line tunnel and dived under the whole layout to emerge on the down side beyond the canal at the top of Camden bank. The tunnel was one of five single line tunnels driven early in the 20th century; the other four were on the newly constructed DC lines at Primrose Hill and Kensal Green. The tunnels were circular, lined with cast iron segments similar to those of the underground network, but to standard gauge as on the Northern City line. It was not possible to achieve electrification clearances through the tunnel, and therefore the upper half of the lining had to be removed, spoil excavated, and a new elliptical upper lining installed. The contractor was Charles Brand, who was contractor to the ER on the Potters Bar Widening.

The work itself was fairly straightforward, and the workforce was very competent. The greatest problem was working wagons into and out of the tunnel. Three working faces were established and wagons had to be changed over each day. New segments were brought in, and old ones together with spoil went out. Cement was also brought in and used to fill the space behind the newly erected segments. An 8F hauled the first train, but afterward the train came in behind a D8000, which left the fresh supply of wagons on the 1 in 37 downgrade outside the west portal of the tunnel, and then ran through to pick up the loaded wagons, couple up, push out of the tunnel and away to Willesden. It was a dangerous place and great care was essential at all times.

Access through the tunnel past the working faces was extremely limited, and it was preferable to walk over the tunnel, of course taking the opportunity to inspect Camden shed and its occupants en passant. It was an opportunity to photograph in locations not normally accessible, so a camera was carried quite often. There was a challenge or two, but once I was known there was no further trouble. It was fascinating to examine the Pacifics at close quarters. As the duration of the contract was over the winter 1961-62 the weather was not on my side for photography. The top of Camden bank was just by the Regent's Canal bridge, and it was a superb location, which I had the good fortune to use on a number of occasions, not unconnected with the sight of a Big Lizzie backing off Camden at 13.00 for the Midday Scot! There were a number of good vantage points in the area, but even though I was able to walk around on-track, it was a dangerous area requiring constant vigilance. One morning I needed to get to the south portal, and whilst near the shed, I waited for the 10.40 Perth. It was freezing cold, with a clear sky and bright sun. My intuition was rewarded by the sight of DUCHESS OF ABERCORN with a big train, with a huge exhaust, gathering speed. It made a superb picture.

Just beyond the canal bridge, beneath the running lines, were the large vaults that housed the winding gear that worked the incline down to Euston. There were four, two for coal storage, and two central ones which housed the pulley wheels, mounted on a trolley so that tension could be maintained in all weathers. At the end farthest from the canal, the boilers and winding engines stood on a raised platform. I believe the coal was delivered by canal and unloaded down a chute into the vaults, and no doubt the water for the boilers came from the same source. It was an enormous installation, and the need for a massive excavation so close to a

The temporary parcels shed at Marylebone takes shape, in 1963. The steel erectors demonstrate the need for the H&SAW Act!

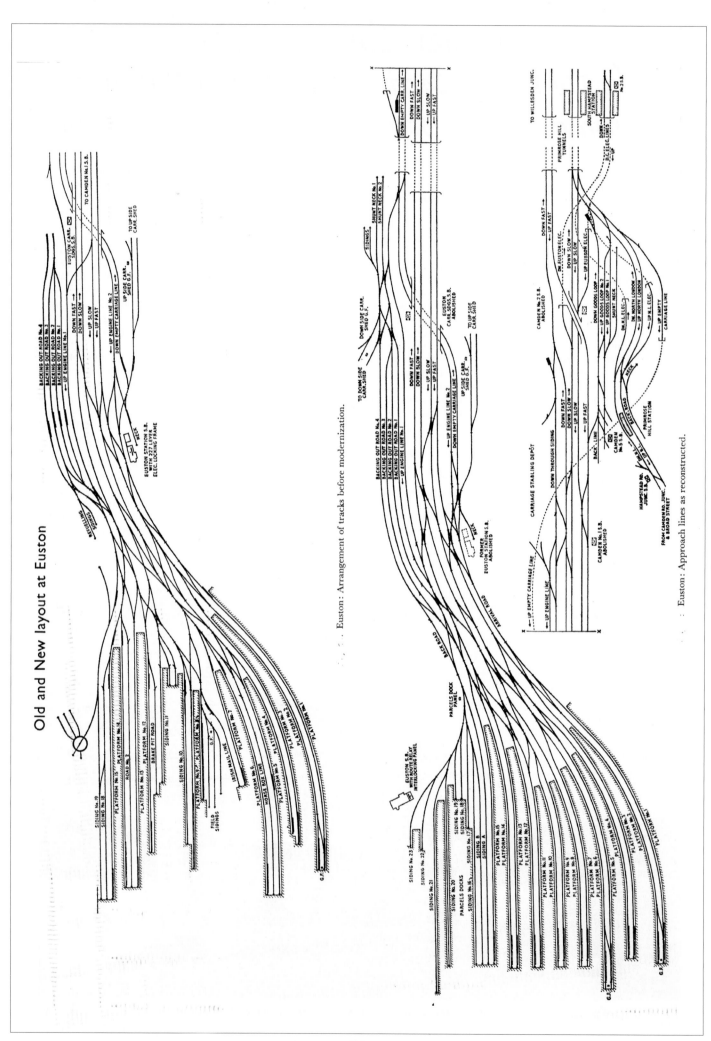

Old and New layout at Euston

. . . Euston: Arrangement of tracks before modernization.

. . : Euston: Approach lines as reconstructed.

Camden Depot in the midst of the 1961-2 cold spell. No.46253 CITY OF ST.ALBANS has been turned and is being prepared for the Midday Scot. A 2-6-4T stands alongside a dead EE Type 4.

Camden up empty carriage line tunnel enabled up ECS trains to leave the up slow, run beneath the Camden complex, and run in at the top of the carriage sidings outside Euston on the down side. To gain clearances for 25kV, the circular cast iron lined tunnel had to be enlarged as can be seen here in 1962, with the ovalised section nearest the camera, and the unrebuilt circular section ahead. Work proceeded using the materials wagons as scaffolding.

Nowadays tunnelling has not so much been deskilled as mechanised, successfully. Altering a tunnel lining is rarely carried out, and it required experience and skill to devise methods to excavate and make room for the new lining, and then to erect the new cast iron lining precisely. Any over-excavation was caulked, and then filled with pumped grout, a mixture of fine sand and cement.

A view of the vaults of the winding engine at Camden in 1962. Eerie would have been an understatement.

Right. Not only did the Camden up empty carriage line tunnel require enlargement for 25kV, but also its portals and the short arch section leading to the start of the cast iron lining. This is the country end portal in 1962.

Below. The elegantly ornamental portal of the original Primrose Hill tunnel, now on the slow lines, in 1962. The double junction joining the Euston slow lines to the Broad Street lines is in the foreground.

PRIMROSE HILL TUNNEL
1182 YARDS

Above. The replacement for the country end portal was formed by continuing the erection of the top section of cast iron lining, and then casting an reinforced concrete arch above. Considering the arch had only to carry the weight of two feet of spoil, looking at the amount of reinforcement 'over design' is the term that springs to mind.

Left and overleaf. Additional views of the work of enlarging the tunnel lining, showing the use of poling (ground supporting) boards to support the ground between the existing and new tunnel lining.

A close up view by the north portal showing two old rings, with the new elliptical rings nearer. The old rings were retaned temporarily for the new rings to be started vertically. The difference in headroom can be appreciated.

The erection of each new ring made use of pulleys, wire rope and an operated winch. The pulleys were bolted into the segment boltholes. care was needed to retain ring plumb; as the old rings were dismantled they tended to spring forward.

Two further views of the work proceeding, illustrating (top) how the London Clay had been cut back by pneumatic clay spades. Below, Clerk of Works Joe Coyle inspects the finished work at the end of an eight hour shift.

working canal must have escalated construction costs considerably. Its presence was rediscovered during the widening of the up empty line tunnel, the vaults having flooded to exactly the same level as the canal. In pitch darkness, with some 12-16ft of water and mud beneath, it was difficult not to feel a sense of apprehension down below. Its relevance to the contract was that during the enlargement of the up empty carriage line tunnel the new crown passed 6ft beneath the floor and no doubt less from the foundations. The presence of such a large volume of water immediately above one's head concentrated the mind sharply. In fact the water above broke through briefly, but the Contractor's staff were ready for it, and there was no further problem. After privatisation the Property Board tried to sell the winding vaults as a potential development for a night club, a laughable prospect for anyone having actually been down there! (Other than the Count of Monte Cristo, perhaps.)

The running lines originally swung round westwards and travelled through the first Primrose Hill tunnel (1220 yards) now used by the slower services. Quadrupling involved provision of a second tunnel on the down side conveying the fast lines. The new, fast lines tunnel was largely straight but with a reverse curve at the east end. The change required the slow lines at Camden to pass through a dip before rising up to the original Primrose Hill

tunnel, while the up fast line flew over them at the dip to reach the newer tunnel. The North London and the freight lines from Camden Goods joined into the slow lines between Primrose Hill and the tunnel mouth, and the up empty carriage line left the up North London to burrow down into tunnel.

Temporary Parcels Depot

With the completion of the tunnel enlargement, I moved on to the construction of two temporary parcels depots at Kilburn High Road and Marylebone Goods Depot. These were required to deal with the parcels traffic outbased from Euston during the reconstruction. Both were hardly much more than simple building tasks. The Marylebone site was in the basement of the old Goods Warehouse that was destroyed by fire during the war. It was sited to the west of the Goods Depot, which itself was west of the station approach tracks. The latter were at a considerably lower level than the goods yard and slightly lower than the basement level. The site access was down a ramp from Lisson Grove under the Goods Depot rail tracks at ground level, which allowed the headroom for a fully laden 9 cu.yd Readymixed lorry. Alas, once the first load was discharged the lorry rose on its springs and could not get out until the tyres had been let down. The construction task was fairly straightforward, but during the preparatory surveying for connecting the new services to the existing, there

was a hilarious episode that bears repetition.

The foul drains from the new depot had to be connected into the sewer that crossed the site from west to east. This was at a low level, so as to pass beneath the running lines outside the terminus. The sewer continued beneath the new diesel maintenance depot east of the running lines before leaving BR property, and there were deep manholes in both the basement site and in the Diesel Depot which appeared to be linked. It was essential to be certain that they were connected and that the flow led from one to the other in order to link the new depot drainage into the sewer. The expert on the local drainage layout was an Irish member of the local Works Inspector's staff. The latter worthy was a proverbial pain, but his drainage man was very helpful. I cannot recall his surname, but he was universally known as Paddy, inevitably. The hut in which his equipment was kept bore the painted name 'The Turd Man'. Both manholes were inspected, and to check the flow a powerful green dye, fluorescein, was put into the western one. Paddy noticed that the nearby toilet block in the Diesel Depot emptied into the eastern manhole, and before descending to check for dye, wisely he closed the toilet entrance. However it was a pity that he hadn't made sure that nobody was already in the toilet!

This was a project in which I encountered the existence of the high pressure water main, which was used

The 11.27 parcels service left Euston station during the rebuilding, picked up additional vans at Kilburn coal yard, and headed north. It often consisted of one box van from Euston. A Stanier Pacific often worked the train, and here is No.46235 CITY OF BIRMINGHAM with its box van leaving Euston on 30 April 1963.

No.46240 CITY OF COVENTRY stands in the old platform 6, known to Euston *habitués* as 'The York', in 1963.

Little did we know that beneath the wheels of No.46240 CITY OF COVENTRY, there was a cast iron three-way wagon turntable. When the platform was closed and the area cleared for the new station, the turntable emerged. It was sent to the NRM but not displayed so far as I know.

to power a number of installations in London at one time. There was an emergency during the project duration, when a high pressure valve casting broke nearby. The contractor was building new platforms at ground level as part of the project at about this time, and I was not best pleased at learning from the Works Inspector that a new platform wall was being built almost exactly on the line of the main, much to his amusement. Moreover, it had been damaged during the war and repaired using welded steel pipe instead of heavy cast iron. Perhaps that worthy had embroidered his story for effect, who knows, but fortunately nothing more was heard about the high pressure main.

On completion, I moved to Willesden for the construction of the District Electric Depot, but after a few weeks of trying to agree the setting-out of the depot with the Contractor in a Somme-like quagmire, I was called back to the Bridge Office to deal with the bridge design for my professional assessment and interview described earlier. I was not sad to leave colleagues out in the mud and rain. Meanwhile the rebuilding of Euston had commenced, and once work in the Bridge Office was completed, it was out into the mud again, and shortly after, a move to join the team at Euston.

During the years following my return from National Service, I was one of a small group that took charge of a number of aspiring civil engineers from public schools on a short introductory course. Few actually joined BR, but the course toured the latest electrification works on stations, P Way and bridgeworks. This was very interesting, and finished with a run from Manchester to Crewe on the inspection saloon, attached to the rear of the Pines Express, running at speeds up to and beyond 100mph. The train started with two new electric locos from Manchester but reached Bournemouth with a 7F 2-8-0 or a 9F 2-10-0!

Euston: The Old Station

Euston was a terminus which recurred several times in my career, as the old station, during the reconstruction, and as a new station, and so there is much to record about the old place. I do not claim that my comments are comprehensive since they are based only on my own experience.

The old London and Birmingham Railway terminus at Euston was opened in 1837, the first main line terminus in London, designed by Philip Hardwick and built by William Cubitt. Located off Euston Road, to the north behind the Euston Square Gardens, there were the Euston and Victoria Hotels (built later), and behind that stood the famous Doric propylaeum, the Euston Arch. I believe it was the largest such structure built in the UK. When the old station reconstruction was initiated, it was necessary to remove the Arch, and the subsequent campaign to preserve it, although unsuccessful, could be argued to be the start of the preservation movement with particular regard to the rail network. The campaign and the subsequent demolition ensured the enduring fame of the Arch.

The Arch was a statement of grandeur and intent. It was a remarkable structure, handsome and imposing, very well built. It was, at £39,000 in 1835, a very, very expensive one. By 1960 it was jet black and its upper rooms were used as what used to be called a muniment store, that is, a plan and document store. It was a pity that the large Euston Hotel block was built opposite, on the south side of Drummond St, obscuring the Arch until close to. It was suggested at the time that it could be jacked up, landed on roller cradles, and moved into Euston Square Gardens. There were examples where this had been done, but the structures involved were smaller and far less heavy than the Arch. It is doubtful whether preservation would have been possible in 1961-62 other than by systematic dismantling and re-erection – for which there would have been neither time nor money. As we found during the demolition, the courses of stone were held together with tenacious lead keys formed by pouring in molten lead. The engineering plant available in 1961 was a very far cry from today, lacking those machines dependent on the development of hydraulic engineering, the use of toughened steel and industrial abrasives for cutting and grinding.

A senior colleague told me a charming story about the Arch. At the regular meeting between the CCE, his senior assistants and the District Engineers

The somewhat ad hoc area between the up arrival and the down departure platforms was known as 'The Field'. The short bay in the centre was used for loading bullion vans, and to the left a 'Big 'Un' stands on the 11.27 parcels. The office beyond the bullion siding was known as 'The Goldfish Bowl', and behind was Bridge No.4, Ampthill Place, now removed.

The departure side before rebuilding, with an EE Type 4 on an express and a Black Five on a Northampton service.

The rebuilding process continues, the Goldfish Bowl has gone and a Watford – Euston DC EMU approaches a new platform.

As related in the text, the driver of the 11.27 parcels contrived to get No.46254 CITY OF STOKE-ON-TRENT 'on the floor' under Ampthill Road bridge. One can see how difficult rerailing was for the breakdown crew. My Clerk of Works colleague obviously had a sense of humour. The lifting pin was left in place just behind him.

SIR WILLIAM stands in old platform 1, with an EE Type 4 in platform 2.

Above and overleaf. 4MT tank No.42430 is coupled on the ECS in old platform 1. As she pulls away, the train loco, No.46251 CITY OF NOTTINGHAM, assists. The train travelled away from Euston on the up side, then crossing to the down side through the flyunder a third of the way up Camden Bank. The ECS was then shunted into the Down Side Carriage Sidings, leaving No.46251 to complete the journey up to Camden MPD.

(DE), the DE St.Pancras (DE London in effect) was delayed due to dealing with a derailment. Freddie Fawcett, referred to earlier, was a good engineer and a good and popular boss, and was one of those people one meets who are slightly larger than life, a character. When a rather overheated Freddie arrived, Arthur Butland, the CCE, greeted him by explaining that a scheme to jack up the Arch and roll it out to Euston Square Gardens had been examined and he had decided to give it his approval. The joke fell flat. Freddie glared around and said 'Well if you're going to play silly b***s, I've got better things to do!' and walked out.

Arthur Butland – ANB to most of us – was a considerable character. The son of a Cornish railwayman, his slight Cornish burr could deceive, since he was extremely sharp and intolerant of fools. I had quite a bit to do with ANB in running the civil engineering students' association, and was often called to the presence. As I got to know him better, I found him happy to answer and discuss intelligent questions, but one had to be on guard. The Resident Engineer (RE) that I worked under at the time gave me a useful hint – ANB had the habit of firing questions whilst waiting for phone calls, etc. It was wise to answer straightaway, since he would question much more closely. 'Don't flannel or he'll have you!' was his advice, and good advice it was. ANB was a good chief.

A colleague with exalted ideas of his ability applied for promotion, and was called to an interview. 'You know the Old Man – what's he like?' was the

question. I repeated what I had been told – don't flannel, answer the question. If you don't know the answer, say so. When he returned, he was not pleased. 'He's a hard man. I thought he was going to throw me out.' I asked what had passed. 'Well he asked me what I was doing, so I told him that I was doing Hampstead Road Bridge, and he got a bit short with me.' I said that the CCE would know that he wasn't in charge, but only an assistant RE. Then he said that ANB 'showed my application form and said "If this is true, you should be on this side of the desk and I on your side."' The rest of us in the site office enjoyed the story.

A far more worthy subject in my view was the Great Hall, opened in 1844, designed by Philip Hardwick's son. A large and impressive hall with a magnificent ornamental ceiling, it lay alongside the western platform 6, always known as 'The York'. Sadly, it could not be saved, nor any part of it, as I enquired from ANB at the time. The reason was that the ornamental ceiling was suspended integrally from timber trusses, which had deteriorated and were becoming dangerous. Of course it was completely incompatible with the new station design. The Great Hall was constructed in soft brick, the side walls of which were 5ft thick at platform level. It was a pity that the Hall could not have been built of better materials to a better and stronger design. Perhaps the L&B had spent too much on their Arch?

The station was small initially, but grew steadily. Built on the corner of Eversholt and Drummond streets,

eventually there were six platforms under a glazed roof. Access for taxis was via an overbridge from Ampthill Square across platforms 1 and 2 and down the taxi road between platforms 2 and 3. The canopy had a wrought iron structure mounted on hollow cast iron columns which served as downpipes to the drainage system. A later western extension provided a number of additional but short main line departure platforms (7-9) and siding roads (10-11) while most of the original platforms were given over to arrivals.

In 1892 further modernisation added four very long platforms numbered 12 to 15, and the large triangular area between the arrival and departure platforms – 'The Field' was occupied with the short platforms, now mainly used for suburban services, loading docks and sidings. By the 1950s the station had become a sprawl between Cardington and Eversholt streets, with difficult road access for mail, parcels and newspaper traffic.

The DE's Works Inspector at Euston at the time was Arthur Knight, a quiet and fairly monosyllabic man who knew every inch of the station, and was a constant source of information during the early stages of rebuilding. Arthur was fascinating to accompany round the station, but his minimal repartee earned him the nickname of 'Silent Knight'. Famously, when discussing some difficult repairs with the DE during a works inspection, a somewhat frustrated FF said to Arthur 'Well, Knight, what do you think? Have you nothing to say?' Arthur's reply was masterly and even

No.46251 lends a hand to push the ECS up the bank. In the foreground the new concrete platform 3 wall is in place next to platform 2 old brick wall. Below, one can see the site service bridge.

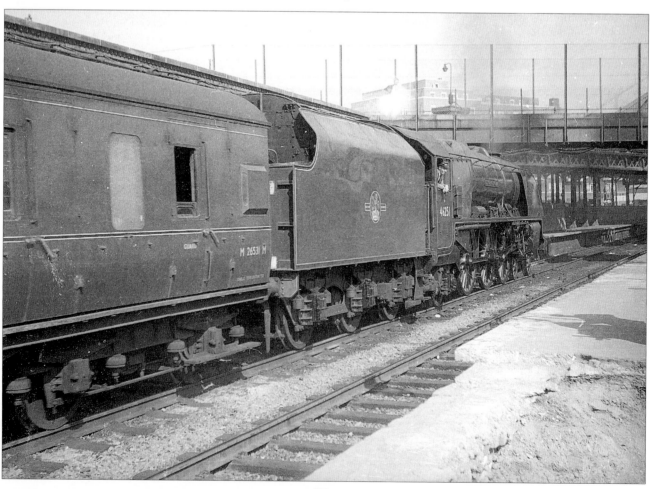

The double headed Ulster Express at Euston, already encountered on page 26.

The fireman on Fowler 2-6-4T No.42350 makes ready to haul his 14 coach ECS up the bank out of Euston. The train engine usually gave a push as far as the platform end.

enjoyed by the DE: 'It's better to say nothing and be thought a fool, rather than to open your mouth and prove it!'

There were a number of bridges around Euston, most of which were numbered 1; that is 1A, 1B, etc. No.1A was the arch carrying Euston Grove across Euston Square Gardens towards the station, used for many years by the Rifle Club. During the reconstruction I discovered Bridge 1F, which was a staff footbridge at the north end of the down platforms, by then roped off as unsafe, a good vantage point for photography for the few steam departures by that time. No.4 was Ampthill Place, which was removed early on, and the first overbridge now remaining is No.5, Hampstead Road, which marks the start of the 1 in 75 bank up to Camden. A small loco depot was installed west of the departure platforms, separated from them by a typical L&B/LNWR glass screen, used by locos off suburban services and ECS duties, and also Jubilees working the Birmingham 'two hour' services. With the introduction of the two LMSR diesel-electric prototypes, 10000 and 10001, a fuelling point was constructed beyond Hampstead Road bridge on the down side, nicknamed 'The Bandstand'. This was situated at the low point at the foot of Camden Bank, and as a result of spillage of diesel fuel, the ballast was heavily contaminated. When p way staff were gas welding worn crossings the ballast was set ablaze more than once.

The Euston-Watford electric services, introduced progressively from 1912 to 1917, used platforms 4 and 5, while the steam operated suburban services used platforms 7, 8 and 9. The ECS working of the latter was unique, I believe. The empty train was propelled up the bank, the loco detached, and the set was then gravitated back down to the correct platform under the control of the guard. It was a particularly dangerous move for staff on the track in the area, with third rail electrified track to contend with, and the lookout men needed to be particularly vigilant. So far as I can recall, apart from the lookout man's horn there was no means of warning on-track staff other than the guard's whistle. Early in my time on the District, P.Way Inspector Max Hampson and Ganger Jim Norton were killed there. Jim Norton had not been above marching in to Euston Grove and making complaints to the CCE personally.

The LM Region, in an early 1950s attempt to bring modernity to the shambles that Euston had become, had constructed, among other things, a new signalbox on the up side north of Hampstead Road bridge, a central office in the station yard for the station operators ('The Goldfish Bowl') and a splendid train arrival bureau on the southeast corner of the site behind platform 1 and 2 and the Left Luggage office. Shortly before I started at Euston, one morning the latter contained an

unusual item of left luggage – 45514 HOLYHEAD, whose driver had been several touches late on the brake with an up sleeper. Drivers descending the bank bound for platforms 1 or 2 needed to control the speed carefully since a sharp left-hand bend existed at the country end of the platform, followed by an easier right hand bend down to the stops. With the vacuum brake, too heavy an application on entering the platform was likely to check the train prematurely. The driver then had to apply just enough steam to keep moving and then bring the train to stand in the usual place, greasy rails and all that.

The Arrivals Bureau was impressive, much the same as a cinema with a set of screens and rows of seats. One could inspect the state of the main line through a glass window from outside, on the west side, and it was fascinating to see the punctuality of the services. Or depressing, if one was a member of the Operating Department. Members of the CCE staff used to habitual late running found it amusing to think that it was such a problem that warm and comfortable accommodation was necessary for those doomed to wait! I cannot recall whether early arrivals were advertised as such, since arrivals BT (early – before time) or RT (right time – on time) were rather less usual, as on much of non-electrified BR elsewhere in the early 1950s. The usual practice was to report RT regardless. In the winter months in a colder world some truly

No.46254 CITY OF STOKE-ON-TRENT gives the ECS loco a helping push out of platform 1.

No.46254 CITY OF STOKE-ON-TRENT rolls quietly down the bank into platform 1. When working on the up side one had to listen carefully for the tinkling of the anti-vacuum valves of the express locos as they descended the bank. Now and again a real expert would come in at speed and bring the train to a halt at the exact spot: one had to be ready and not be caught unawares.

The Stanier Pacific Railtour brought a large number of enthusiasts to Euston – and a certain amount of chaos. Here No.46245 CITY OF LONDON stands at Crewe.

'The glory hath departed'. Euston before rebuilding, and below, during the demolition of the arrival side as it moves closer to platform 6.

amazing delays were announced, particularly with the Anglo-Scottish overnight services, running into several hours at times, especially the Royal Highlander. I remember at least one occasion when the Highlander arrived during the lunch hour!

Euston: Modernisation

With the implementation of the 1955 BR Modernisation Plan came the electrification of the West Coast Main line from London to Liverpool and Manchester, and within the overall electrification plan was the reconstruction of a number of main stations and the modernisation of the remainder. The two largest were Euston and New Street, and I was closely involved with the former at the outset. The old station at Euston desperately needed radical alteration in order to cope with electric traction and an increased service with up to 16 coach trains. To accommodate the traffic displaced from Euston, the temporary parcels depots already

referred to were constructed at Marylebone, in the massive goods warehouse area that had been devastated by fire decades before, and in what was once Kilburn coal yard. Some passenger traffic was diverted to both Paddington and St.Pancras.

When the new terminus was opened in 1968, architects and self-appointed aesthetes queued up to criticise the design, and the received wisdom was that it was and is a disaster. In reality BR was in a sense the Government's kept woman, largely dependent on state funding. BR's remit and financial authority was for a new terminus and not to create a national work of architectural merit. Whether it should have been was not for BR to debate. Some might feel that it was as well that it wasn't! It worked as a terminus and in any case there was far more to it than that. The original intention was to rebuild the station and at the same time develop the site commercially, including a hotel block. On that basis, a

comprehensive contract based on a cost plus approach was agreed in 1961 with Taylor Woodrow Construction. Cost plus was a form of contract in which the contractor implemented an agreed programme of construction, and the client paid the agreed costs of the work plus a profit. It was and is used where time is short, the task is not clearly established, and the contractor is used to contribute to the design. It needs careful control and good relationships. The danger is that the client's mistakes are costly, and contractor has no incentive to question the need for work and method. These contracts were unusual on BR, the preference being for traditional contracts that were properly measured, costed, tendered and controlled.

The problem was that the authority for the project, which in view of its size and funding, lay with the Government of the day. It was an early time for large commercial developments, and there was considerable debate over whether the state should be involved. Eventually, when the contract had started and a deal of work had been undertaken, the senior minister responsible, in rare moment of sobriety, decided against development, thereby wrecking the approach on which the project had been planned. As a result Taylor Woodrow's incentive had gone, and they withdrew many of the senior staff, since the contract was now simply a station reconstruction, albeit a large one. In retrospect, they produced a good station, but whether it was value for money I cannot say. I believe that TW were compensated for loss of profit, but it was a long time ago now.

The contract now required the construction of eighteen passenger platforms; four for parcels and other traffic, a parcels depot above the platforms, and a somewhat *de minimus* station building. The parcels depot was carried on huge underreamed bored piles, as I recall, 3ft in diameter, some 80-100ft deep and the base expanded to 10-12ft. For the hotel block, which, at the time of reconstruction, had not yet been cancelled, several groups of sixteen bored piles, surmounted by huge pile caps about 24ft square and 6ft thick, were provided down the line of the old taxi road. They are still there, unused. I remember that the excavation of one huge pile cap exposed some cast ironwork in the corner. It was with a sense of alarm that we realised that it was a Northern Line tunnel!

Work started with the construction of a main sewer on the up side, and the clearance of the signalbox site on the down. A temporary overbridge was erected from the taxi entrance off Eversholt Street, across to Cardington Street on the down, which allowed access ramps to be added or removed as work continued, enabling plant and materials to reach different parts of the site. As far as I can recall, old platforms

The faded glory of the Great Hall in 1963.

Right. Demolition moves into the central area of the old station.

Inset right. The old arrival platforms 1 and 2 were kept until enough new arrival platforms were complete, and then they were rebuilt. Here a 22RB piling rig starts to bore a one yard diameter bored pile, which would in due course form part of the foundations of the extended parcel depot deck.

Left. The demolition of the Great Hall progresses. It was the demolition of the next section that caused the Royal duststorm referred to in the text.

Below. The steelwork erected, the reinforcement begins to take shape for the parcels deck. In the distance the old Cardington Street offices and dining club remain.

The floor of the parcels depot comprised pre-stressed concrete planks as *in situ* formwork, overlaid with an reinforced concrete slab.

The reconstruction of Hampstead Road took place along with the reconstruction of Euston. Removal of the old bridge involved lifting out the old main girders, and in view of the capacity limit of the contractor's crane power, it was judged necessary to lighten them by cutting 'windows' in the web, as here. In fact it made little difference and the rest of the story is in the text.

1 and 2 were kept in use, possibly 3 as well, and the rest of the arrival side platforms were demolished in order to put down the bored piles and start constructing the new platforms. During the demolition, a three way cast iron carriage turntable was found beneath the stops on platform 6, which is now at the NRM. Also, it was somewhat disturbing to see how easily the cast iron columns of the old roof broke. From the cross-sections it was obvious that the central sand core had been disturbed during casting, so that the wall thickness of the columns, which should have been uniformly one inch, actually varied eccentrically from ¼in to 1¾ins in many cases.

Most of the demolition work was achieved by 22RBs with a long jib and a demolition ball – the 22RB was the 'Black Five' of the plant industry. For the demolition of the Great Hall shell, the walls were far too high for the ball to be used safely, and so a rather crude method was used. It caused a hilarious scene. A large bulldozer had one end of a wire rope attached to it, and the far end was then passed level into the Hall, taken up and passed over the top of the wall back to the dozer, to which the second end was attached. The dozer was placed clear of any falling masonry, and so it set off gingerly, and the wire rope tightened. We waited for the crash, but no – the wire simply cut through the soft brickwork like a cheesecutter through, well, cheese. Retreat, adjust the wire rope – which was heavy – and try again.

Meanwhile, into one of the remaining platforms – 2, I believe - came a gleaming Black Five with a gleaming, unique train. Yes, the Royal train. On site, we had not been advised of this and in retrospect one would have thought that we should have been. The railway of the mid-20th century had many Berlin walls. Work carried on. Then Police appeared from everywhere, plus an army of BR bowler hats and polished black shoes. Meanwhile, our friend with his bulldozer was still battling with the wall of the Great Hall. This was under TW's control, if control is the right word, and I was the assistant RE on duty. A police officer, looking alarmingly senior with an appropriate amount of braid, came over and told me to stop work on site until the train had gone. I passed the instruction immediately to TW's foreman, but before he could make contact with the driver above the roar of the dozer engine, finally the wall gave way with a tremendous crash, the dozer scuttled clear, and the whole of the up side of Euston was enveloped in a great cloud of London & Birmingham Railway dust. I doubt whether a single uniform or bowler hat escaped. It was difficult to keep a straight face. It was just as well that the Royal train was safely platformed well before the arrival of the Monarch, allowing the rather dusty members of the welcoming party to recover their poise!

The signalbox foundation comprised 360 bored piles, about 12ins in diameter and some 20ft deep. The method of boring was primitive, using a heavy steel cylinder with a cutting edge, dropped from a tripod frame. Even in those days it was painfully slow, and since the clay contained many boulders, I know that hardly any of the 360 are straight and most are badly curved! As the piles were friction piles rather than bearing their load, bearing capacity was probably improved. Since the signal box has served us well for half a century, we can be thankful for factors of safety and over-design! The large piles on the station site were bored by a crane-mounted auger, and the shafts were examined before concreting. Now it can be revealed, that on inspecting one of the pile shafts, I bequeathed my National Service boots to puzzle the archaeologists of the future, before the ready mixed concrete was poured. Station operation was heavily curtailed, but during the day I kept an eye on departures. There were two Birminghams, 8.45 and 16.30 as I recall, usually the haunt of a Big 'Un, and I managed to capture a few shots. Trains such as the 10.40 Perth were usually diesel hauled, but now and again the diesel had been failed and a Pacific was standing in. No longer did the Midday Scot have the occasional Pacific in charge. One sunny morning Frank Bennett's 46245 CITY OF LONDON had been supplied from Willesden shed and it was a treat to see this gleaming loco come pounding up the bank with a heavy train. One had the feeling that things were changing though, such as when DUCHESS OF HAMILTON set off with the 8.45 Birmingham, lost her feet half a mile out, and rolled her train back into Euston for a second try, this time *with* the ECS loco banking.

There was an 11.27 parcels service that left 'The Field', which was often hauled by a Big 'Un. The train looked utterly ridiculous, consisting of a Pacific hauling one box van, but extra vans were picked up at Kilburn and Brent. The platform exit was protected by an arrangement that I had not seen

The old Euston. Demolition has started. One of the best ideas of Taylor Woodrow was the service bridge which linked both side of the station, with attachable ramps down to the platform areas.

As demolition proceeded, part of the old London & Birmingham station were exposed, such as these cellars.

Euston demolition. A view across the site showing the portion of old roof over platforms 1 and 2 left *in situ*, and the start of new platform construction.

elsewhere. *As I recall*, to give flank protection against sidelong or conflicting movements in a very confined area, the two switches of the trap point facing the driver were worked separately and could act as a double tongued trap, i.e. both switch blades could stand open instead of being linked by tie bars. All was well so long as the driver didn't move against the shunt signal. One morning, the driver of 46254 CITY OF STOKE-ON-TRENT did, and the momentum of the Pacific carried him forward into the mass of ironwork under Ampthill Place bridge, with disastrous results. Most of the departure side was shut all day as the breakdown crew struggled to find a foothold for the lifting jacks, since the loco was upright but use of a crane was out of the question. Eventually 46254 was restored to the track late in the day, and having been kept in steam, was moved back towards the loading dock whence, etc, etc. Alas, a lifting pin had not been removed from the frame between the coupled wheels, and the connecting rod was not the same after half a revolution. I remember the tirade from the Loco

Inspector on the subject of ruining a perfectly good loco. Fortunately she was repaired and I enjoyed my last journey with a Stanier Pacific behind her in August 1964.

Construction of the platforms progressed westwards, and the remaining old arrival platforms 1 and 2 were demolished once new platforms were available. The infill between platform walls was spent ballast, recovered from p. way reballasting operations on the LMR. This brought us into contact with the p.way organisation, which at the time functioned rather like the Wild West in its more colourful moments. The delivery of the promised number of wagons loaded with spent ballast occurred as the exception rather than the rule, and the air was often heavy with threat when early in the week only a fraction of that number turned up. Sometimes the spent ballast came from Districts well beyond Rugby, which made it very expensive fill indeed. Of course TW's machines were waiting, expensively, to unload and spread the expected infill. Possession was nine-

tenths of the law, and wagons were a vital commodity. The new track layout was designed in 95RBS bullhead, and it was laid in by the CCE's and District Engineer's organisations. A number of new platforms were equipped with a continuous trough, similar to water troughs, with a water supply to flush the troughs into the foul drainage system. This was a requirement laid down by the Camden Borough Council to combat any health risk, for the overnight sleeping car trains were intended to arrive much earlier and stand in the platform until a civilised hour. In fact whenever I used them, the sleeping car trains were platformed on the west side of the new station, and in the days of Mk.1 sleepers I can imagine some dissonance on the part of p.way staff regarding track inspections and maintenance.

While contractors were, in my experience, decent people, occasionally one ran across someone in the company who had seen everything and knew everything, a relic from the civil engineering Wild West. This type of John Wayne character took advice from nobody, and could be told nothing. Such a man was the general foreman of a contractor working on the renewal of Hampstead Road overbridge. One day I found him, with a man cutting holes in the web of the main girder. (See illustration page 80). He was lightening the girder prior to lifting. Aware of the fact that a crane's lifting capacity reduced sharply as the jib was let out from vertical, I advised him that he would need a very large crane to lift as planned, but cutting out web panels would not reduce overall weight by any more than 3-5%. My advice and relative youth were flung back smartly, and I was told to make sure that the contractor's possession requirements had been agreed. They had.

Shortly after I moved to the station proper and thought no more about it. A month or so later, on a Monday morning, the Euston site office were in hysterics. The road crane had arrived at Hampstead Road bridge, and the driver either couldn't or wouldn't go for the lift. The foreman therefore had instructed that the girder be cut in half, *lengthwise along the central, or neutral axis*. The crane supported the girder, but the lower half, now deprived of the strength of the top flange, flopped gracefully across the up side tracks and blocked the up side of Euston. Meanwhile, the very unstable top half flapped about trying to fold itself in half. Fortunately all up tracks were under possession at the time. It always pays to listen.

Once a sufficient number of piled foundations had been constructed, work on the structural steelwork for the canopies and the overhead parcels depot was started. This was followed by the construction of platform walls, infilling, and then surfacing. Then the remaining old arrival platforms were removed, and

The parcels deck takes shape at Euston. In the foreground is one of the ramps from the service bridge.

work on track remodelling could be started. Meanwhile, other electrification works were under pressure, and I moved into the Direct Labour organisation.

Some years later, when a service was still in operation on Christmas Day, the Area Manager, on call, chose to visit the staff at Euston. The station was deserted. He was in the Travel Centre talking to staff, and the vast concourse was empty. In those days it was not yet the Persian market our major stations have become. Then, a young couple entered the deserted concourse and looked around. The public address system was playing pleasant music, they looked at one another, and waltzed round the concourse to applause from the Travel Centre!

Camden Bank

Although not strictly part of the Euston Station project, the incline to Camden and the Camden area were closely connected and so I have included it as part of the Euston area. The first 1¼ miles to Camden No.1 signalbox was a fearsome start in steam days. Robert Stephenson is said to have originally planned to build the terminus at Kings Cross, but an impasse with landowners resulted in the alignment as today, with a long and heavy curve from Primrose Hill tunnel turning south to Euston. As

Below. At Camden MPD No.46228 **DUCHESS OF RUTLAND is about to move off to work a northbound express, 1X76. It is January 1962, in the grip of a very cold spell with new diesels failing for one reason or another, and the Stanier Pacifics were having a brief return to the 'front line'.**

More of the emerging Euston Parcels Depot.

Left. Hillhouse engine shed, at Huddersfield, had a freight turn that brought one of its three Class Fives into Willesden with astonishing regularity. At the time I had no idea where on earth Hillhouse was. Standing at the top of Camden Bank on a freezing cloudless sunny morning in February 1962, a Class Five came up the hill with the ECS of an overnight sleeper, bound for Stonebridge Park. The loco was No.44780, one of the Hillhouse triumvirate: the other two were 44948 and 44949.

Below. On one of my trips through Camden shed in 1961 I was surprised to see Royal Scot No.46133 THE GREEN HOWARDS, once one of the Holbeck locos which worked north from Leeds to Carlisle and Glasgow. The paint was clean below the thin layer of grime, suggesting that No.46133 would be well run-in by the time it returned to Holbeck!

Before the cold snap I was able to photograph a pair of 'Lizzies', No.46203 PRINCESS MARGARET ROSE and No.46206 PRINCESS HELEN LOUISE at Camden in late 1961. Already they were becoming scarcer on the main line.

No.45647 STURDEE heads toward Primrose Hill Tunnels with her freight in April 1962.

A gleaming new DP2 stands at the top of Camden bank, having worked its first train from Liverpool to Euston. The following night it was put in the London end of the shed, now converted into a little diesel depot, at which point the examination track opened up and DP2 sank to the floor!

The 12.05 'Red Rose' blasts up Camden bank in May 1962 behind No.46242 CITY OF GLASGOW. The boiler appears to be priming, but otherwise there is no leaking steam despite the loco working very hard with a big train.

The 14.10 express freight to Crewe pulls out of Camden yard in May 1962 behind Royal Scot No.46159 ROYAL AIR FORCE double-heading Class Five No.45191.

with all four north-facing termini, the Regent's Canal proved to be a difficult obstacle. The GNR went underneath, but the other three crossed over. St.Pancras was constructed on an arched undercroft to raise it sufficiently to cross the canal. The track out of Marylebone rose to cross over the canal. The London and Birmingham Railway was faced with the need to lift its metals more than 70ft in just over a mile in order to cross the canal. The first half mile actually fell to pass beneath Hampstead Road before starting the climb. The severity of the 1 in 75 gradient was always said to be too much for contemporary steam traction, justifying the existence of the Camden winding engine and cable operation. In fact there was a legal restraint since neighbouring landowners insisted, notably The 3rd Baron, Lord Southampton, that the Act authorising the L&B prohibited the use of steam locomotives south of Camden down to Euston. In fact the winding engine was taken out of use in 1844 after only seven years of operation. Presumably the prohibition of steam operation from Euston expired with the L&B at the end of 1845. Or possibly with Lord Southampton? In fact the 1 in 75 was a simplification, and at its steepest the gradient was 1 in 70.

The 1892 modernisation resulted in a considerable enlargement of facilities on the bank. It must have been a major project. Ampthill Place was Bridge No.4, and Hampstead Road and Granby Terrace formed overbridge No.5/5A at the foot of the bank. With electrification

it was necessary in the 1960s to provide 25kV clearances beneath the bridges, and so No.4 was removed and Nos.5/ 5A were rebuilt. As mentioned earlier, the CCE had set his face against track lowering for electrification. In the case of No.5/5A the road profile allowed sufficient lifting. The railway itself was widened considerably in the 1892 works; bridges were rebuilt to a wider span and a short tunnel constructed.

Large carriage sheds were built on both sides of the line and, as I remember, that on the down side was used for main line sets while that on the up side was used for suburban sets. In 1960s the down side carriage shed had to be re-equipped completely with the necessary clearances and services for electrically hauled stock. This project was completed by the Direct Labour Organisation (DLO), referred to later. There were a number of through sidings between the running lines and the down side carriage shed, used for ECS prior to dropping down to the station. The tracks either side of the line were on a flatter gradient, and the four running lines rose steadily above them. The headshunt on the down side was by Park Village East, surrounded by retaining walls of considerable height. A flyunder enabled ECS to be withdrawn from the up side and travel to the down side where it could be stabled in the down side carriage shed. The engine and ECS tracks continued north of Park Village East at an even steeper gradient on the down side. A new box, Camden Carriage Sidings, stood above the

intersection bridge. By 1953 there were six tracks serving Euston station yard. The central pair were the slow lines, also used by the DC electrics, while those on the west were the downs and on the east, up lines. The westernmost and easternmost lines were also used by ECS leaving or arriving at the station, as I recall. The central four passenger lines rose up to Camden; down fast, down slow, up slow, and up fast.

Beyond the intersection bridge the running lines entered Bridge No.8, which was really a long overbridge rather than a tunnel, beyond which lay a quarter of a mile or more to the top of the bank. By the 1950s it carried a major road intersection and commercial premises, which presented considerable difficulties when the bridge had to be raised to achieve 25kV clearances. The raising and rebuilding of Bridge No.8 was one of the more advanced tasks for electrification. The down side abutment wall was parallel and very close to the eastern retaining wall above Park Village East, and in order to strengthen the abutment, the space between the walls was excavated using bentonite slurry to maintain stability, and filled with concrete. The rebuilding was also a complex task involving temporary support work, and had to be carefully programmed to keep traffic moving above.

The ECS and engine lines on the down side passed through a conventional tunnel in parallel to but (continued on page 94)

Sir William himself stands on Camden shed after coaling, in 1962. No.46256 SIR WILLIAM STANIER FRS was one of the hardest working 'Big 'Uns', fitted with roller bearings, as was sister Pacific No.46257 CITY OF SALFORD.

89

No.46251 CITY OF NOTTINGHAM standing at Camden in 1962. She may have been withdrawn by then. It is interesting that the Stanier Pacific, a very large machine, looks even more imposing with the fill-in valancing ahead of the cylinders.

No.46156 THE SOUTH WALES BORDERER leaves Euston during 1963 with the 16.30 for Birmingham.

D289 thunders up Camden Bank with the 'Red Rose', a heavy train. Not as inspiring, though, as a steam loco.

No.46239 CITY OF CHESTER, well turned out for the 'Midday Scot', starts the descent to Euston. Here the tracks have reverse running, since the up Engine line is on the right, and the down Engine/ECS line is on the left.

4MT 2-6-4T No.42099 on Camden turntable, 1962.

Camden's rebuilt Jubilee No.45735 COMET on the turntable, 1962.

Ivatt No.46456, working on ECS, at Camden shed in 1962.

Hornby-Dublo's post-war No.46231 DUCHESS OF ATHOLL at Camden.

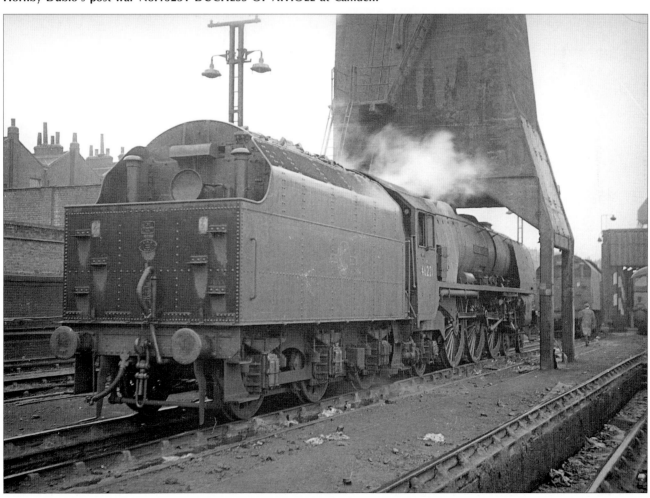

lower than Bridge No.8, and beyond they were joined by the up empty carriage line, already mentioned. Having reached the top of the bank, the tracks crossed the canal underbridge. Beyond on the down side was Camden Motive Power Depot, while on the up side was the massive Camden Goods Depot. The latter had a large storage area underneath for goods awaiting transfer to local trips or onward transport by canal. In the early 1960s large numbers of bales of wool were still stored, and the area positively reeked of ancient fleeces.

The canal bridge at the top of the bank was followed by the heavy curve referred to earlier. The running lines originally swung round westwards and travelled through the first Primrose Hill tunnel (1,220 yards) now used by the slower services. Quadrupling involved provision of a second tunnel on the down side conveying the fast lines. The change required the slow lines at Camden to pass through a dip, flying under the up fast before rising up to the original Primrose Hill tunnel. The North London and the freight lines from Camden Goods joined into the slow lines between Primrose Hill and the tunnel mouth. The up empty carriage line left the up North London to burrow down into the tunnel referred to earlier. The single track tunnels for the DC lines at Primrose Hill and Kensal Green, and for the up empty carriage line were all bored and lined with circular cast iron segments as referred to earlier.

The MPD was the main express steam depot, code 1B, home to both types of Pacific, the big 4-6-0s, Jubilees and Black Fives, and ECS classes. It was not as large as some main London steam depots, and appeared to be squeezed into the site on the down side, inside the left-hand curve from Euston round to Primrose Hill tunnels and bounded by Gloucester Avenue. It was home to express engines in the main, and certainly I had the impression that there was not a lot of space to be had. Walking through the depot was far less hazardous than along the running lines, and left one with a vivid impression of the sheer size of the Big Lizzies. In the harsh winter of 1962/63, the depot had a number of failed Type 4 diesels waiting attention and the sad sight of a number of withdrawn Pacifics.

The workshop at the London end of the depot building was an early conversion to a small diesel shop. The rails were mounted on a series of short reinforced concrete columns (stools) to enable access low down on the loco or underneath. The Region was still examining the Deltic, which appeared on Liverpool services now and then, but one evening I was astonished to see a new diesel loco, DP2, the Class 50 prototype, with an up Liverpool express. On the second evening she ran light up to Camden, and was moved to the workshop for examination. As she moved slowly in, the road opened up under the loco with disastrous results for DP2. Either the driver braked too hard, or the concrete stools were structurally inadequate, or a bit of both – I have long since forgotten. Many years later, Bill Tyldesley, an old friend, was reminiscing about his time during the 1939-45 war when I believe he was Running Foreman at Camden. He, like many others at the time, was under great pressure to keep locos running and at the same time get the basic servicing completed. One of the problems was the time taken to return locos to steam after washout at busy times. Bill was nothing if not an innovator, and realised that a length of used boiler tube with a gas connection would make a rather large gas poker, fed off the gas lighting system. This was used to build up a good firebed quickly and start to raise steam much more quickly. It was important not to reheat the locos too quickly of course, so judgment was essential. It worked well. However, at the regular Euston District management meetings, the District Goods Agent at Camden Goods complained frequently about the varying gas pressure, which often fell so low that it was difficult to see in the gaslit offices, let alone read and write. Suddenly Bill realised why.

With the end of the steam era, Camden Depot was replaced by a fan of sidings for stabling A/C EMU units, and with the loss through reorganisation firstly the Sundries traffic, and then wagonload traffic, the vast expanse of Camden Goods Depot and Yard slowly but surely became the housing and industrial estate that it is today. The arrival and departure loops on either side of Regents Park Road bridge have been replaced by service roads gaining access for road vehicles.

No.46241 CITY OF EDINBURGH has stalled with the 10.40 Euston-Perth by the down side carriage shed, due to inadequate assistance from the ECS loco, which was supposed to provide banking assistance. After setting back (see page 149 also) No.46241 was successful second time around.

No.46252 CITY OF LEICESTER, withdrawn, at Camden depot.

No.46254 CITY OF STOKE-ON-TRENT waits at Euston on the 11.27 parcels.

The underside of bridge No.25, Scrubs Lane bridge looking east, the usual chaotic mess arising from the lack of space on site. The tracks in the foreground led to Willesden District Electric Depot, then under construction.

The large main girder spanning the four running lines. Its twin blocked the WCML (briefly) when being lifted.

Chapter Four: On Site with Direct Labour

The Direct Labour Organisation (DLO) on the LM Region was a device for the employment of temporary staff under the supervision of permanent BR staff. The organisation was deployed from the CCE's New Works Office in order to carry out new works projects on track or structures. The electrification had moved into its final stages, with pressure on all resources. Locos, wagons, cranes, manpower, and possessions; all were in heavy demand by the CCE, CS&TE, and the CM&EE's Electric Traction Engineer (ETE). As a result scarcely a day passed without incident. I had been asked to move to the DLO to cover a vacancy, which quickly became a permanent appointment.

There were three centres, Stonebridge Park (London), Camp Hill (Birmingham) and Manchester, with a London sub-office at Leighton Buzzard. The quality of work by the DLO was good. It tended to be expensive because the projects passed to the DLO were not always well prepared, often with difficult access and in some cases the nature of the work would have been a licence for a contractor to print money. At the Stonebridge Park office, the workforce was overwhelmingly Irish, while at Leighton Buzzard, it was largely local men. The staff were temporary BR employees but paid at rates set by the building industry. It was marvellously flexible, and I was acting as a contractor within the BR organisation.

The first problem was that, without any training or instruction, I had, from anticipating and instructing others, now to do it myself. Not difficult on the face of it, but I realised with some abruptness that unless I took the decisions, made the arrangements and gave the instructions, nothing happened. Like the rugby or soccer coach, it is one thing to say what should happen, but entirely another matter to get on the field and do it!

I had five gangs on different projects. In the largest gang of 18, the steelfixer ('Walsall Jack') and carpenter (Frank) were English, and the rest were from the west of Ireland. The foreman was Patrick Joseph Conlon, a native of Roscommon, a strong, swarthy man. He struck a daunting figure with his crew cut and a deep voice, but this impression rapidly disappeared as I found Pat a firm friend and an able colleague. As a unit the gangs were cheerful, hardworking and well organised, and very good to work with. Tommy Holleran's gang actually conversed in 'The Gaelic', and while friendly and polite, I was never quite part of 'the crack', the general chatter. The crack was one of the great pleasures of working with the country Irish. On one occasion at Hallowe'en, it rained heavily all day, and Pat's gang fell into exchanging ghost stories. As each man spoke it must have triggered memories in others, and it was fascinating. Oh, for a tape recorder!

An initial minor problem was my unfamiliarity with the broad Irish accent. Pat took me round the site and then we went into the site hut, where the teaboy, one Colman Fahy a cheerful man from County Clare, was asked to make a cup of tea. 'The kittle is laking, and the schtove is out' was his reply. After a few attempts, I realised that the elderly kettle was the problem, as was the antique coke stove. One of the great advantages of the DLO was that I had a triplicate order book and the authority to use it. No works orders in triplicate! I made out an order for a large gas boiling ring, a new kettle, and a couple of gas cylinders from our suppliers, gave it to Fahy and told him to take the van and get them. A gang without tea was no good to me. This had never happened to him before, for the tradition was that teaboys scrounged for their bits and pieces. He was very impressed with the gas ring and its ability to boil rapidly: 'By Jeez that's a quare yoke, so it is' was his comment. Henceforth I could do no wrong! Also, I was beginning to understand the dialect. So began a period which was as enjoyable and rewarding as any in my career, and that was in part due to the people I worked with.

Colman was a delightful character, unconsciously amusing, who provided my first encounter with the rural Irish.

Bridge No.25 Scrubs Lane. The pipe bay, below the new pavement, which will carry electricity cables, water mains, BT and other cables, and in some cases gas mains and drainage although not here.

A general view of the site with a Type 2 approaching bridge No.25 on a parcels train. One of the LMR's two 50 ton cranes stands on the bridge. The general mess was typical of WCML in 1964-5.

A trip to remove spoil wagons with Willesden's oldest 0-6-0 diesel shunter. The London side of the bridge has been removed and the abutments have been raised to the new headroom.

Bridge No.25: On this day, all Willesden could spare was an 8F, No.48018, for the trip. The DC lines to Euston are in the background.

I was taken aback by the quaintness of his language, coloured by his Roman Catholic background. For example, when I asked the whereabouts of Pat, the reply was 'I declare to the Lord Jesus Christ I have not seen him this hour past'. Often a reply would be prefaced by a religious protestation. As I had no driving licence at the time, I had a driver, Jack Conlon, who was Pat's brother. Both Colman and Jack had a fluency and humour that was uniquely and delightfully Irish, and their observations and stories gave me a pleasure and fascination of which they were quite unaware. Many of the others were similarly good company, and one feels that a good television career eluded some of them. The one characteristic that the gangs shared was a love of horses, racing and betting, almost ad nauseam. Much of the conversation – the 'crack' – debated the relative merits of jockeys, trainers and their nags. I forget the exact details of the races, horses and odds but I have quoted representative figures. There were the fantasists who boasted of having a string of racehorses back in Ireland. I remember Jack, glasses on the end of his nose, reflecting, after losing his usual weekend bets, that 'Vincent O'Brien took two donkeys to Paris, so he did.'

As a reader of The Times, I suggested to Jack that he could read my newspaper for tips. After all it was said

to be the top people's paper. 'Begod, so it is' said Jack, 'It's Ascot next week, and your man will be in the know'. Seeing Jack studying The Times was one of many happy scenes remembered. When I asked how he was getting on, the reply was that 'Your man couldn't tip himself out of bed'. On another occasion, at Bridge 23, we arrived during a shower of rain, and went with the gang into the hut for tea. Tommy Holleran and most of his gang were deep in serious debate – the Derby. I forget the horse that was favourite for the Derby – Sea Bird, I think – but I remember that Jack told me that it wasn't worth backing as the odds were bad. 'A man would be buying money, so he would' was his verdict. With a strange Irish logic he was considering backing another horse with better odds.

Jack joined the debate by declaring that Sea Bird was as good as past the post. The horse couldn't lose. Everyone agreed, but the lookout man, a West Indian, Sam, thought that it could lose. After all, there were upwards of two dozen horses in the field. The argument developed to the point where Jack planted a fiver on the table and declared that Sea Bird would win. Sam laid a fiver on it, and Jack laid another fiver. I was mildly apprehensive that this was getting stupid. Eventually the two agreed that if Sea Bird won Jack would take £40, and if any of the other 20-30 horses won,

Sam would get £40. Tommy held the stake. In the van I ventured the opinion that things had got out of hand, but Jack grinned back. 'Your man would only give me 6 to 1 on. That's buying money. This way I've got an even money bet.' And of course he won.

One project required the ground to be prepared for the new District Electric Depot (DED) track layout at Willesden. The main carriage shed used to be to the east of the high level station as referred to earlier, between the main and DC lines. It was demolished to make way for the DED. The original survey contained an error that suggested that the area between the tracks was larger than it actually was. Work had been completed on the depot drainage system before the mistake was found. The amenity block had been started by the Regional Architect, allegedly in the wrong place, but on checking, much to the CCE's chagrin, it was proved to be correct and even worse, the track and drainage layout being laid in was in the wrong place. When the revised layout was complete, the drains were *under* the tracks rather than between, and the catchpits had to be reconstructed to allow maintenance access from between the tracks. This was good example of the sort of job which would have been very expensive with a contractor. Staff shortages and the rapid increase in the number of engineering trains had caused

The deck beams of the new western half of the widened Bridge 25 showing the shear connection reinforcement.

Work proceeding on cleaning the abutments and piers, ready for raising to electricfication clearences.

Bridge No.25: A closer view of a main pre-stressed beam. Single line traffic travels over the newly erected western country or side of the span.

obviously a strengthening LMS vehicle, had clouds of blue smoke pouring from the rear axlebox. One had to think carefully about intervening in the operation of the working railway, but here there was no doubt, and so I went to the signalpost telephone to alert the signalman.

A voice answered: 'What d'you want?'
'The last coach of that down express has a hot box'.

The response astonished me: 'What am I supposed to *** well do about it?'
'Send seven *** bells before it comes off the road!'

Clearly this call from a stranger had interrupted the signalman's moment of quiet reverie. Or perhaps he was having his lunch. It was a good job I had no idea who the District Signals Inspector was.

Most of the work was bridge reconstruction or lifting. To achieve the necessary clearances for 25kV electrification, most of the overbridges were wrought iron or steel girder bridges, and required reconstruction. Many were four track spans since all four tracks were at six-foot spacing, and the constructional depth of the new prestressed concrete structure was less. Where the road surface could not easily be raised, reconstruction was an attractive option. In a few cases where bridge condition permitted and increase in headroom was no more than a foot or so, the structure was lifted. Originally the intention was to take advantage of the reduced clearances required for 6.25kV electrification in the London Area, but the 25kV clearances were revised down, and it was decided not to step the voltage down to 6.25kV. I believe there had been problems in the Manchester area with the reliability of the APC (Automatic Power Control) magnets, which changed the locomotive power control system to accept the lower voltage.

Farther north, Direct Labour gangs were employed to demolish arch bridges and replace with either shaped in situ RC arches or PC decks. The technique employed involved demolition of the parapet and spandrel walls together with removal of the road surface and the in-fill beneath. The arch bridge was thus reduced to the arch ring, provided it was structurally sound. In the first case the arch ring was used as formwork, carrying lightweight concrete shaped to form the soffit of the new RC arch. It was then coated with a release agent, and the new RC arch was cast on the back of this assembly. Once the design strength had been developed, the old arch was drilled and blown down by a carefully controlled explosion. Use of explosives was carefully supervised and controlled, but for all that, hilarity was never far away. There were some embarrassing incidents caused by a partial demolition, wherein blocks of the old arch and lightweight concrete remained suspended beneath the new

numbers of newly recruited goods guards to appear on engineering trains. One arrived with an engineering train on the up slow at the Euston end of the DED layout during the midday meal break with a train of second-hand rails. At that time most but not all of the area intended for the DED track layout had been covered with spent ballast. This was ballast recovered from weekend relaying which included degraded ballast and spoil, which formed a good sub-base. Later the track was laid, fresh ballast unloaded and the track was lifted through it and fettled. At the time the DE had laid the S&C fans at each end of the DED, and one through road through the depot linking the entrance and exit. The engineering train was intended for the through road in order to unload materials. The guard, obviously a new recruit, beckoned the driver back with a rolled-up newspaper, from the brake veranda on the outside of the curve from Kensal Green tunnel and barely

visible to the crew. The guard had failed to check the lie of the road as the 1950 Rule Book required, indeed he remained on his brake. As the road was set into a large hole as yet unfilled with spent ballast, the train was propelled off the road into the hole. The guard seemed transfixed as his brake dived off the road, strongly reminiscent of the captain going down with his ship, impervious to the shouts of everyone around. Frank Bennett, the Willesden Shedmaster, reckoned that the busiest loco on his shed was coupled to the breakdown crane, in action most days. He put the prototype diesel 10001 on the job, one of her last, to avoid keeping a loco steamed up.

One of the sights at Willesden was the occasional appearance of a Big Lizzie. Three were at Willesden, immaculately kept, but now and again another appeared. The down 'Red Rose' came out one day hauled by a Pacific, and as she roared past, the last coach,

Above. Bridges consist of two parts – the substructure and the superstructure. Here, unusually, we can see the former without the latter. The eastern or 'London' half of BR.25 is being prepared for raising.

Left. A hired 60 ton Lorraine crane has placed the temporary sling beam, which supported half the main span while the other half was removed. The crane is the same one which blocked the WCML for a nerve-wracking period. This time it had the slings hired as well! In this view, looking towards Acton, the service bridge, now complete, is on the right. The sling beam is behind the old main beam. The web plates have been cut to facilitate attachment of the lifting slings.

Bridge No.25: A closer view of the connection between the sling beam and the main crossbeam holding half the road, which was still open to traffic. The main crossbeam was cut by thermit lances.

arch despite liberal coatings of release agent. That necessitated extended possession of the line while the recalcitrant lumps were prised loose very carefully. Meanwhile operational chaos reigned and the CCE had to field more than a few searching questions from the General Manager.

The second alternative required demolition of the arch ring. The abutments were then raised to the required height, new bedstones placed or cast, and the inverted PC tee-beams were placed to form the deck. The beams were then used as the formwork for an in situ concrete deck which combined the bearing capacity of the beams into a single slab, on which the parapets and

road surface were constructed. I must admit that I did not supervise directly the first form of bridge renewal, but the prospect of a five-brick arch ring standing alone with traffic passing beneath, without any TSR, would have taxed my nerves more than somewhat. That view was reinforced during a conference at the Institution of Civil Engineers at which the Camp Hill RE reported that one of his arch rings on the Trent Valley line had collapsed without warning not long after an express had passed. Once again the line was shut for several days while the rubble was cleared and while suitable responses to even more searching questions from a high level were

demanded. I remember that the RE seemed to find the episode amusing, unlike the eminence of CCEs sat in the front row glaring at him.

With the old local government boundaries, three overbridges in the Willesden area, in less than two miles, were administered by three councils, each with different specifications and standards for the same work. This was a time of small municipal minds and too much authority. At Queens Park the Bakerloo Line emerged from underground, joining the DC lines before the station. There was a carriage shed beyond the station for the Bakerloo trains terminating there. Salusbury Road Bridge No.20 at Queens Park had already been renewed in concrete and was simply raised. The DC lines continued through Kensal Green tunnels, and then swung out round Willesden South carriage shed and BR. No.25 to the Junction station. Bridge 23 (Chamberlayne Road) was between Queens Park and Kensal Green, and it had to be rebuilt with prestressed concrete beams. The simple task was made far more difficult as two huge TV cables ran under the pavement on the Euston side. The problem here was to rebuild the bridge round the cables without touching them. The cables were carefully suspended from a temporary beam and the existing bridge deck was removed. The new beams were erected and everything was going well, and when the last beam was lifted, while I went down to release the materials train, Pat decided to slue the cables a foot or so to enable the last new beam to be erected. True, it would have been impossible to land the last beam otherwise. 'We were very careful' said Pat. 'Sure it'll make no differ'. If TV reception had been ruined in the area, I imagined that a nearby bridge reconstruction would be the last thing to be blamed!

The biggest gang, Pat's, was working on the reconstruction of the overbridge at Scrubs Lane. It consisted of three spans, one over the DC lines, the next over the DED entrance, and a 58ft main line span. Before work started, however, the gas and water services, both of which had large mains over the bridge, had to be diverted over a separate pipe bridge. In order not to miss a possession in which one of the rail breakdown cranes had been booked, the six long prestressed concrete beams were erected on scaffolding towers, since the supports themselves hadn't been completed. Completing this work was complicated, working inside the scaffold cage. When it came to rebuilding the bridge, the two smaller spans were well within the capacity of a hired road crane, but the main span was too heavy.

Then came the blow. The LMR had two 50 ton road cranes, massive machines for the 1960s, and the one booked to me for the main line span

Bridge No.25: A close-up view of the ends of two main beams showing the lifting hooks and the anchorages of the pre-stressing bars. The strip of material is the bearing pad, made of special hard compacted material.

The old Willesden South Carriage shed has been demolished, and the site is ready for construction of the Diesel Electric Depot and its sidings.

My favourite shunter at Bridge No.25. No.10001, one of the prototype diesel twins of 1947.

was taken for emergency repairs. The chances of hiring another from a plant firm were nil. Then I remembered that the other 50t crane was at Euston, and glory be, it was not being used until the weekend after. However, my colleague said 'You move it'. That meant getting police authority and a route, since it was a wide load, and that was only forthcoming when I had obtained verbal agreement to the specified route from every local borough council, utility, water board, British Waterways and all. At least the WI was not involved. My colleague's estimate was at least two dozen telephone calls.

Now Willesden required a good telephone system to function at all, and that centred on the manual exchange on the approach road. The operator at the exchange was an elderly lady who was regarded as somewhere between difficult and impossible, depending on whether she had been sworn at and by whom. This lady had BR Willesden by the vitals and ruled it with a rod of iron, and woe betide anyone who was less than deferential. It could be a very long while before they got their call. In a moment of inspiration, I decided to anticipate trouble, and went to see the

lady at Willesden Exchange, and explained that I needed to make some three dozen telephone calls to get this crane to Willesden. She promised me every assistance and was as good as her word. Ne'er a hard word passed my lips. Thirty six calls later, I met the police sergeant at Euston, and off we set with outriders as far as Camden Town. An outrider reported that Kentish Town Road was blocked to us by a series of sewer headings, and so with a muttered obscenity the sergeant led us off on an entirely different route! The lady at Willesden had a box of chocolates for her trouble, and I never had any problem with phone calls from then on! An older colleague had observed that 'it is wise to bow gracefully before the inevitable – a little oil helps the wheels go round!'

The bridge was rebuilt in two halves. A large temporary steel girder was used to support a half width bridge while the other half was demolished, widened and rebuilt. The girder arrived at Willesden well before the time when it was needed, and to guard against it not being available when needed, it was sent to a colleague at Rockcliffe Yard, Carlisle, who returned it in time. There was also

considerable delay in the delivery of the prestressed concrete beams from Newton Heath concrete works. Nine 27 ton concrete beams disappeared without trace for over three weeks, and it was only due to the experience of my Clerk of Works that they were found in time. He located them on the stops at Cricklewood far from the scrutiny of the aged number snatcher.

The demolition of the existing bridge caused me a few nasty moments. Having stripped out the jack arches, we were allowed to take possession of the slow lines and a between trains possession under Rule 217 (T2 in the new Rulebook) with a 40mph TSR on the fast lines. That meant that when a train was offered on the fast lines, the signalman needed the confirmation of the Operating Inspector on site that work had stopped and the line was unobstructed before clearing signals. I was using Thermit lances to cut out the wrought iron secondary girders, which were partly encased in concrete and brickwork. Thermit lances were steel pipes with iron wires threaded through, heated to near white hot while a mixture of oxygen and acetylene was blown through. This released a large and very

Willesden MPD in October 1963. Rebuilt Jubilee No.45736 PHOENIX stand alongside Britannias Nos.70043 LORD KITCHENER and 70052 FIRTH OF FORTH. The two rebuilt Jubilees, Nos.45735 and 45736, were known by many on the LMR as 'The Heavenly Twins'. They were so much better and more powerful than the unrebuilt locos. In retrospect it is a pity more were not converted, for they would have galvanised the Birmingham and Midland services.

Willesden's 'Jinty' 0-6-0T No.47307 shunts at the back of the shed, in October 1963.

Frank Bennett's pride and joy was his group of three 'Big 'Uns', which were kept in immaculate condition, like CITY OF LONDON here, in 1963. Willesden and Camden men also called them 'Big Lizzies' to distinguish them from their older sisters, the 'Lizzies'.

hot flame which would cut steel, concrete and brickwork. Each girder to be removed was carefully slung from a road crane to hold it level and safe from dropping on to the tracks below while each end was cut free. When free it was lowered on to the materials train below on the slows.

When a train was due on the fast lines, the District Inspector stopped work and gave permission to the signalman to clear his signals. On an instruction 'One on the up, stop work', the Thermit operator immediately shut off the oxygen and we stood back until the train had passed below. In fact the particular girder only needed a few square inches more cutting to be free, and those inches were red hot. The operator should have completed the cut before giving the District Inspector clearance, but having shut off, reigniting the lance took time. We all watched, horrified, as while the Merseyside Express went slowly past, the remaining metal snapped, and the smoking girder end hung there to astonish the passengers. 'If your man Beatty (CCE Bill Beatty) is on that train we're in quare trouble, so we are.' observed Pat.

Having got the secondary girders out from the DC lines and DED entrance during the week, the main girders of both smaller spans and the 60ft 27 ton girder spanning the main line were removed at the weekend. The plant hire contractor, Greenham, had hired a new Lorraine 60 ton road crane from a sub-contractor, Mechquip, and so we were all set. We removed the two smaller main girders, and we moved to lift out the main girder. It was a simple task: lift, swing through 90 degrees and lower, jibbing out, on to the bogie bolster in the materials train beneath. At about 2am I asked the driver to get the slings to attach to the big girder, to which that worthy replied 'What slings, Guv'nor?' This was certainly not what I expected. Nobody hired out a crane without the means of picking up, but due to some quirk of the insurance world, this sub-contractor did, requiring slings to be hired – and no doubt insured – as a separate contract and no doubt cost. This had not happened before with any crane hire contracts. Now I was well and truly stuck.

Well, to cut a long story short, I decided to lighten the girder by cutting windows in the web between the stiffeners, although in truth it was more cosmetic than effective. Having got the Greenham plant hire manager out of his bed and acquired three 7 ton slings, I went for the lift. Wrong. Ropes were attached to the girder so that once the crane took the weight, it could be rotated slowly as it was lowered. However, the crane driver, anxious because the jib was well out and his crane was now over maximum load, lowered the girder before the men controlling the girder could rotate it sufficiently, with the result that it was now firmly wedged between the abutments. Even wronger – the WCML was now firmly blocked with a girder jammed across all four roads. The crane hadn't the capacity to lift the girder as it was jammed. The Wylie alarm on the crane, set to warn the driver of excessive load on the jib, was going continuously despite the cloth cap wedged to silence it. So was the driver, somewhat hysterical since his back wheels were about to lift off the ground. After sizing up the situation, another rope was attached to the girder at the down fast end, then tied to the corner post of a brake van hauled by a D8000 diesel. The driver was then instructed to inch – and I meant inch – forward. Amid splintering noises from the brake, and yelling from the crane driver, it swung free. The men pulled it to line and it was lowered quickly on to the bolster. At least 50 workers, officials and bystanders on site started breathing again! All of us on

Willesden, by late 1963, was servicing a number of visiting Pacifics; No.46235 CITY OF BIRMINGHAM and No.46228 DUCHESS OF RUTLAND sit it out among the freight and shunting classes there.

A relief to the down 'Red Rose' approaches Willesden behind No.46240 CITY OF COVENTRY. Bridge No.25 was a superb photographic vantage point.

No.46240 CITY OF COVENTRY heads (as I recall) the 17.05 Euston-Blackpool in place of an EE Type 4.

electrification works were under heavy pressure not to miss out on our programmes, since possessions and plant were committed every weekend, and the dates for wiring were not far away. It had been made very clear that to jeopardise the wiring dates was more than a departmental matter. The GM was said to want the miscreant's head on a plate – colourful exaggeration but it left one in no doubt as to the urgency of the situation. Nearly everyone in civil engineering has a crane horror story; this was mine, my fault but I had got away with it. I could think of several colleagues who didn't, and turned the crane over. I resolved that next time, there wouldn't be a repetition. I would stop the job regardless until the correct equipment was available. I often wondered quite what the Carriage and Wagon Dept made of the slightly rearranged brake van.

When the second half was ready for erection, the weekend possession had been agreed and the Willesden 75 ton breakdown crane was booked. This time another trainload of concrete beams had arrived at Brent without incident. Meanwhile an inspection of the bridge nearby carrying the North London lines at Willesden High Level revealed a need for immediate strengthening. The weekend's work was disrupted by the breakdown crane

being taken, along with the temporary supporting girder, to deal with this emergency. I had finished with the girder and it needed to be removed, but could ill afford to lose ten hours of the possession without the crane. Worse still, the new deck was isotropic, although mercifully not transversely prestressed. The new beams were of classical I-section, and had projecting reinforcing steel stubs down each side of the flanges so that when each beam was lifted into position, the stubs meshed, and the intervening gap had to be filled with high strength concrete as a shear connector. I had heard about these shear connectors being difficult to erect. The stubs had been bent here and there while being loaded, shunted and bumped about. Getting a beam to mesh with its neighbour was like mating two hedgehogs, and an unsavoury college rhyme sprang to mind. Lowering and positioning 27 tons of beam is one thing, without having to swing it sideways and then disentangle it for another try was another. Not for the last time did dear old Ireland come to my rescue with sledge hammers and brawn.

When the crane arrived at 10.00, and while she was being prepared the position had been explained to Willesden Shedmaster Frank Bennett. He was acting as banksman with his depot crane and said simply 'We'll see

what we can do.' The banksman was in sole charge of the crane and its driver, and only he could instruct the driver. Nobody else. Frank announced to all that if he heard any other whistles, he would do something insanitary with them. I had never seen a steam crane worked like it: the crane driver was a veritable Bill Hoole, a full regulator man. I have no idea whether steam cranes had a type of hammer blow, but as each beam was lifted, the pounding of the crane was reflected in the slight bounce of the beam on the slings as it rose quickly. Standing on the newly erected beams, I could feel them bouncing with the pounding of the crane, transmitted through the clay foundations and abutments. We had made such good progress that the whole bridge erection was completed in half the time allowed. Apart, that is, from another incident, operational and potentially serious.

The crane stood on the up fast, and the materials train was on the down fast. A 'Between trains' possession under Rule 217, now T2, applied to the slow lines. If the signalman wanted clearance for a train from the Site Inspector, before it could be given, any crane move had to be completed, the crane swung straight and secured. Therefore getting clearance took far longer. The materials train had been moved up by the DE's representative as the beams were lifted

An up express drifts past Willesden District Electric Depot, under construction on 9 June 1964, behind one of the few rebuilt Patriots still in service, No.45530 SIR FRANK REE. One can see the temporary arrangement of tracks in order to serve the site with spoil, then ballast, and finally track, as well as materials for the depot itself.

An interesting, appropriately named but not terribly useful shunter at Willesden, Jubilee No.45733 NOVELTY, once of Bushbury depot and the 'two hour' Birminghams.

off and placed, and the loco, at the Willesden end, was almost on the Willesden South S&C. In the midst of getting clearance, it was moved again, without the signalman's authority, and it tripped the track circuit on the S&C. This happened during a request for clearance, and distracted the signalman and District Inspector in the signalbox. As a result the approaching ECS, which should have been stopped on the down slow, was allowed into section without confirming that the line was clear – which it wasn't! The detonators alerted the driver of the 2-6-4T hauling the Royal Scot ECS, and he pulled up less than 200 yards from the crane. That was one joint enquiry that I had no involvement in, thank goodness, but I gathered that it involved a spirited exchange of views to put it mildly.

At the country end of Willesden Junction main line station Old Oak Lane crossed the main line on Bridge No.26. The bridge was probably in steel rather than in wrought iron; it was in good condition and it had been decided to lift it. Before a bridge could be lifted, the services crossing the bridge – gas, water, electricity (power and lighting), and sewerage – had to be identified and adapted by the appropriate authority to accommodate the proposed lift. Getting public utilities to act in concert rarely worked, and so work started in cutting trenches carefully across the road to establish the position of the service routes, and to expose the girder ends, backfilling temporarily with gravel. It was my experience that one never dug up a pavement without finding a surprise. The electricity authority had a device which was attached to an unidentified cable, basically a copper blade with an explosive charge to drive it into the cable. This was fired from a safe distance by pulling a cord. The demise of London's tramway system had left a number of unidentified heavy cables under the pavements, most of which were dead, as was that on Br.26.

Being close by the Willesden telephone exchanges, both GPO (as it was then) and BR, it was not surprising that a large number of telephone cables were in the bridge. These were carried in ducts protected by concrete, and so the GPO was invited to locate and mark the duct route precisely. This was done with great care. Pneumatic drills were then used to break out the road concrete, starting *well* away from the GPO route. Billy McHugh put the very first drill straight through a telephone cable. So much for accurate records! The GPO staff spent weeks on site repairing the cabling. Otherwise the job went well. The road was closed during the lifting, and by now, my colleagues and I having experienced the variety of ways in which Murphy's Law impacted on bridgeworks, I wondered what else might go wrong. In fact the lifting went smoothly and the girders rested on trestling while the bedstones and bearings were raised. Then the girders were lowered into the new position and the road was resurfaced to its new levels.

Willesden Junction was and is an important node point on the main line to the north. On the down side a trailing junction brought in the West London Line from Clapham Junction on the LSWR through Kensington Olympia, and almost simultaneously another junction led to the North & South West Jct line at Acton Wells, which gave access on to the GWR at Acton through another connection. With the construction of North Pole Depot for the Channel Tunnel, the use of the direct link from the West London Line to the former GWR main line ended, and services were diverted to Willesden. From the West London the services were directed straight on to the link through the SW sidings to the N&SW at Acton Wells, now upgraded to passenger standards, and down to the Western. On the up side the electrified North London Line passed overhead, with the High Level station immediately above the main line. The line continued west on a girder bridge and divided between a link to the West London line, and the electrified North London line continuation to Richmond via the NSW link to Acton Wells. The closure of the main line station enabled the realignment of the running lines and rationalisation of the S&C layouts.

On the down side beyond the station was Willesden steam Motive Power Depot. It was strange to wander the old place legitimately after the schoolboy years of illicit visits. The Shedmaster Frank Bennett, who, apart from being custodian of the interesting steam locomotives on shed, was in charge of the breakdown crane. He also had three

The 11.27 parcels stopped at Bridge 25. No.46239 CITY OF CHESTER was held at the home colour light signal, mounted on a gantry actually within the enlarged bridge structure.

Premier power for the Scots goods. No.46251 CITY OF NOTTINGHAM runs light, tender first, to Camden Yard to pick up 4S68, the Camden-Crewe fast freight.

Big Lizzies, 46239, 46240 and 46245, which were well cleaned and in good condition. While he tried to ration their mileage, for fear of having them withdrawn, drivers were aware that a Pacific was there for the asking. They occasionally appeared on the 17.05 Blackpool, although it seemed that Frank was not above sending a Britannia instead. I daresay the firemen were not impressed. It was essential to agree the site arrangements for the bridge reconstruction with him, and to have plenty of the civil engineer's cure-all – old sleepers – on hand. After the splendid work on Br.25, on the basis that one should make your appreciation known to people who have put themselves out for you, I wrote a letter of thanks to Frank. Apparently he had never received such a letter before and, suitably incredulous, put it in pride of place in the notice case! It was one of the sadnesses about the old railway that Berlin Walls prevented proper communications between departments. Contact with the Motive Power department seemed to be confined to complaints about drivers' speeds or over the shortcomings of the track. Knowing drivers and firemen as an enthusiast, I made a point of travelling with them frequently to hear about the state of the track.

The following week I was allocated a shunting loco. Having laid in the District Electric Depot (DED) drainage, I had to organise more spent ballast to complete a level surface for the DE to lay the DED trackwork. The loco was required to shunt loaded wagons for unloading on temporary tracks and then remove them. As a gesture of thanks, Frank promised me a good loco. I am sure, Dear Reader, you will understand my astonishment on Monday as a 9F stopped by the site hut on the up slow, and the driver called out 'Loco for the engineers department.' I was hoping for a 350hp diesel shunter, but I had got the biggest freight loco on shed. I suppose I might have got one of his Big' Uns if one was in steam. The driver was reluctant to do any shunting since the reverser on the 9F was stiff, and hard work. Alas, that is all that there was. Cups of tea and diesel oil resolved the situation but I was glad the Garratts had been withdrawn by then.

Having renewed the bridge, profiled the road with weak concrete to provide a smoothly curved vertical surface and laid the tarmac, it was time to move on. Two unsought extra tasks were handed down, firstly the base and holding down structure for the driving simulator at Willesden DED, and secondly a new signal gantry by Br.25.

Both involved placing concrete in awkward places, a problem eased by a ganger's trolley that appeared out of nowhere. That was the great thing about Pat's gang, useful things would be 'borrowed'. Pat was impressed that the gantry dropped on to its holding-down bolts effortlessly, but having used a few, I knew that they were nothing if not a little flexible! Again, with an excellent if disconsolate chippie, with confidence I could cast the holding down bolts suspended from his accurate formwork in the simulator base.

Occasionally I needed to deal with one of the northern gangs from Leighton Buzzard, for one reason or another. On one occasion Jack and I went to pick up some equipment, and I was surprised on entering the hut to see a few pheasants hanging behind the door. Johnny Betts was the ganger, a young Buckinghamshire lad, and he was a crack shot with a catapult. The bridge adjoined an estate that was bristling with gamekeepers, and one could see the birds from the road. Jack's eyes were like saucers – 'Oh Jesus if only a man had the two barrels tucked behind his seat there'd be a fine supper'. John explained that a shot would give the game away, but a catapult was silent and, in his hands, deadly. I remember him gratefully for a tip he gave me, namely that concrete vibrators work better with a cupful of diesel oil poured down the poker tube.

On a never-to-be-forgotten March 15th, in a fit of generosity, I offered to take Pat to a nearby pub for a celebratory St. Patrick's Day drink to recognise the effort he had made with the bridge reconstruction. Strangely, he demurred. Then the penny dropped. He had intended to take the gang for a drink, and so I extended my invitation. Well, I had got myself into this, so I had to make the best if it. It was a happy time. Never had I seen Guinness and beer pass over the bar in such quantities. Worse still, I had failed to remember the courtesy of the Irish, who insisted in reciprocating, every man! Not intending to consume 18 pints, I excused myself more than a couple of pints on the grounds that I had to go on track in the afternoon. It got worse, beer became

whisky, and an alarming line of glasses on the bar formed an alcoholic challenge. Pat came to my rescue, quietly emptying the row of measures into a bottle. He presented the half bottle of whisky to acting teaboy Andy McIntyre, who in our absence had safeguarded the hut and made the tea. He drained the bottle on the spot!

The position that I held was originally advertised as requiring someone who could drive, and not having passed the test, I was sent on a driving course at The Grove at Watford, the old wartime LMSR HQ bought pre-war from the Clarendon family. In the outbuildings the Road Motor Dept had a driving school, where its drivers were trained on a variety of antique vehicles, most of which predated the invention of synchromesh! After a day on a three-wheel Scammell Scarab I graduated to a 3 ton flatbed lorry with no traffic

indicators and one driving mirror, the size of a shaving mirror. My instructor was an Ernie Wisbey, a man who had retired from the heat and burden of the Goods and Cartage department. He was generally known as 'Whizzo', highly inappropriate for a very nervous man for whom 20 mph was the absolute speed limit. I spent several days as a one man traffic jam creeping along the A41 with a frustrated mile of cars behind me before graduating to the school's Austin A55. The latter was an elderly saloon that was still bouncing a mile after it hit a pothole, but the driving instructor was superb. The high point was driving a Scammell Scarab and trailer down Park Lane in London – at 20 mph of course – a frightening experience with taxis and buses flying past on both sides.

A fellow pupil, who had spent years driving Scammell tractors around in St.Pancras Goods Station, managed to put the fear of God into Whizzo... Now, the three wheel Scammell tractors had a rather ineffective foot brake, plus two hand brakes, one for the tractor and the other for the trailer, either side of the vertical steering wheel. The whole arrangement seemed reminiscent of mechanical signalling. Driving a tractor and trailer through Watford under Whizzo's supervision, my friend approached a zebra crossing, and, seeing an elderly lady on the crossing, slowed down. As she reached the central road island, he accelerated, but the lady about-turned and came back. My friend let go the steering wheel to grab both handbrakes while slamming his foot on the brake, but Whizzo, misunderstanding his motives, leapt out!

The next task was a busy overbridge at Highbury Grove over the North London line which needed renewal. I had received no plans so far but the gang was moved and the site hut was set up. While plans were awaited for the new bridge deck, we set about investigating the contents of the services ducts under the pavement. These proved to be even more of a Pandora's Box than usual. The slabs of the closed eastern pavement were being lifted when Pat drew my attention to a cast iron notice on the wall. Cleaned of a century of filth, it warned of a CEGB 132kV cable protected by steel plate under the pavement. Pat's reluctance to go anywhere near it was understandable; in addition, the CEGB would need to be consulted before any work was done. The DE, for whom the renewal was being undertaken, agreed that we should move to the western side while his office dealt with the CEGB. Having gingerly restored the eastern pavement, the western one was then closed off and the slabs lifted. Below the bedding sand was concrete, across the pavement. A walk round the area surrounding the bridge revealed no less than Highbury Telephone Exchange to the north, and the manager there told

From BR. No.25: The new DED is taking shape in the background as CITY OF CHESTER moves away to the north. Stanier's pacific looks just as impressive at this angle as from the front.

me that there were 43 large telephone cables, in ducts set in concrete, crossing the bridge. The reconstruction would involve independently supporting both the CEGB and the (then) GPO cables, and rebuilding the bridge around them. The DE had not anticipated this major complication, and ordered a shut down for further consultation and redesign. From a cursory inspection it didn't look too urgent a renewal to me.

We then moved on to renew the (now) Thameslink span at Kentish Town, a refreshingly simple task cheek by jowl with the cellars of a pub! It was notable for two reasons, the first being the proximity of a pub and its cellars, and the second being the proximity of surely the last of the old-fashioned stationmasters. To a gang 95% Irish, the first was more good-natured humour. Spike Milligan contended that while most people develop a thirst, the Irish are born with one. Although most of the gang could sink a few pints, middle age had brought with it a degree of sobriety. The stationmaster marked his territory by referring to 'my station' and insisting that any work on 'his station' required his permission. He was well known – indeed notorious – in the District. The man was entitled to be consulted if work affected the passengers – of which there were few – and I agreed to that. Otherwise he was directed to a handful of senior operating names from my days at St.Pancras should he feel hard done by.

Although much of the work was bridge reconstruction there were other types. A bank slip on the down side at Hendon was one. It had slipped before, and the standard treatment was counterforting, which involved cutting deep trenches up the slope at right angles to the tracks and filling them with large broken rock or lumps of slag. This time I had to construct a sheet piling wall at the foot of the slope. The presence of large blocks of slag from the counterforting made it impossible to interlock every sheet pile as normal, and I was not given enough possession time to remove them beforehand. Excavating at the foot of a slip was not a good idea, anyway, as it would destabilise it further. The blocks prevented the piles being driven on a smooth line, something that the new DE Leslie Soane pointed out to me. A wag in the gang offered to withdraw them and drive them to a proper line, but I doubt Leslie saw the joke. This was a chance to use the Dalmag hammer, and it put the piles down splendidly well if not quite perfectly to line.

Another slip had occurred at Wembley Hill due to seepage from an underground reservoir up the hill. The prescribed solution was a concrete retaining wall for which ground had been excavated in sections as I recall. The site was well away from the road, which made concrete pumping the only feasible option to deliver a considerable volume of concrete where it was required. Pumping concrete was in its infancy on BR, and we were learning. A fairly basic system had been set up. It consisted of a large hopper beneath the overbridge into which the ready-mixed concrete was dropped through tubes (elephant trunking). A long pipe led from there to the point of delivery, where it was deflected down into the formwork. The pipe was full length at first since we worked back towards the station. A large compressor charged a reservoir, and once the hopper lid was secured air tight, a valve was opened from the reservoir, and the concrete was blown down the pipe to be placed in the formwork.

Learning was messy. Occasionally the pipes parted company and concrete was placed anywhere but where it was wanted. Sometimes the compressor refused to start – as was in the nature of compressors. The hirer had laid great stress on the need to wash the equipment after use, and this was achieved by blowing water down the line at the end of the day. To loosen any concrete lining the pipe walls, we needed to blow a 'ferret' down the pipe with the water, the ferret being a ball of sacking bound with barbed wire. On the first occasion, the deflector was removed and the end of the pipe raised clear of the fresh concrete. A ferret had been manufactured, but it must have been a trifle overlarge, since repeated charging with air had failed to move it. Eventually the ferret went, like a shot from a gun, heading strongly for the shires, never to be seen again! The work proceeded well, but I believe a smaller ferret was used subsequently!

One of the worst tasks was the modernisation of the down side carriage shed at Euston. The walkways between the roads had to be replaced with RC

Royal Scot No.46155 THE LANCER, working a railtour through Rockingham. This was one of the last to be hauled by a Royal Scot in BR service.

A train of ECS bound for Stonebridge Park enters Willesden behind Black Five No.45391.

plank units, but the task had no drawings to indicate quantities, and as time went by, the job grew larger. Water supply points at 60ft intervals were required, and electricity shore supply points were added. The existing walkways were earth, and so each one to be cleared, then drainage, a foundation layer and, the service routes laid, service posts concreted in and the new walkway laid. We had one road blocked at a time. Tommy Campbell's gang started the work, supplemented with a pair of bricklayers from the Leighton Buzzard office. Despite his Scots name, Tommy was as Irish as Guinness, and his gang were good. The electricity supply was a later addition, but an even later one was the decision to replace the LNWR timber panelling of the eastern side with a single brick wall. As the ancient woodwork was removed, the 25kV equipment being installed was alarmingly close. Scaffolding was placed outside, but before a great deal of new brickwork had been made, work was halted. A group of ETE (electric traction engineer) inspectors came on site, walking through to check electrification clearances and anyone working near the overhead line equipment (OLE). They were astonished at seeing men working near 'live' equipment. In the rush towards energisation the Direct Labour Organisation had been overlooked, and we had not been warned. Of course it

was not live but in future it had to be regarded as live – common sense. So my bricklayers had to work overhand from inside, but the quality of their work was super.

I was apprehensive at the task of instilling a fear of the live equipment into the gangs, but I was greatly assisted by a pigeon. One evening in the down side shed, the OLE was now live, and the gangs were working away. Pigeons tended to roost, some on the contact wire. One bird, taking off, stretched its wings, reduced the gap between the wire and the roof girders causing a flashover, and a violent explosion. A single feather slowly floated downwards, there was a general chorus of *Bejesus*, and a few crossed themselves. Message understood.

We were running out of time and as I was anxious not to have one of those interviews with the General Manager Henry Johnson, I pulled Pat's gang in on a second shift to supplement Tommy Campbell's gang. The work went pretty well, although the New Works Office added the odd manhole or catchpit to keep us busy. The plumber was a character, Fred Bishop, a Londoner who would have been speechless if his hands were tied together. The then Metropolitan Water Board had stood Canute-like against the march of plastic, but since the supply came from a large storage tank and not directly from the mains, Fred was allowed to use plastic.

The eternal optimist, he was nothing if not confident, despite not having used it before. Came the great day, water was turned on. Pat's view was that it was like the fountains of Rome.

In January 1966 through running with electric locos was commenced and trial running started. One morning, going to the District office at Watford, I caught the 8.30 from Euston a decade or so after my first acquaintance, but this time there was a Doncaster-built 25kV Bo-Bo on the front. Euston was a shambles at this time, and our departure was fifteen minutes or so late. What followed was a revelation. Camden bank no longer existed, as we accelerated up and shot round the curve into Primrose Hill tunnels. By Willesden we were up to 100, and reached 105 at Harrow, and ran into Watford right time! As drivers were restricted to 75 mph and instructed not to run early, the Operating Dept Inspector at Euston wanted to know which train had transgressed, but I affected not remember. It would have been a poor reward for initiative for the driver to receive a 'Please explain' letter.

My last task was another bridge, at Junction Road junction, the scene of the Old Testament deluge some years earlier. Within days I learnt that I had been successful in applying to join the new London Division at Watford, and so a very happy and eventful period in my training had come to an end.

The trusty Dalmag piling hammer carried by a 22RB (if memory serves me aright). It was driven with diesel fuel, and the crane would haul the piston up in its frame, sending a charge of fuel into the chamber at the same time. On release a piston dropped, compressing the fuel:air mixture, which exploded sending the piston up and the pile down. If the weather was cold, it would refuse to fire straightaway, but a shot of ether would make the hammer fire – and how!

Chapter Five: Divisional Life

In the mid-1960s, there came one of the reorganisations which befell us at an increasing frequency for the next 25 years. Districts were merged into Divisions, and with adjustments to the WR boundaries, the LMR had grown to 14 Districts before it metamorphosed into seven Divisions. The new London Division was formed by uniting St.Pancras and Northampton Districts under Leslie Soane, the DCE. The West Coast main line boundaries were at Brinklow and Brandon on the Birmingham line, and Oakley on the Midland. The GC was closing north of Calvert, and much of Northampton's secondary routes had gone with Beeching's axe.

The WCML was now electrified and operating at full speed, and the Midland was run mainly with Peak diesels and DMUs. The WCML had been relaid with CWR north of Willesden with various fastenings on the main lines, and CWR was now appearing on the Midland. I believe the Chief Civil Engineer, W.F. (Bill) Beatty, had agreed to hold off TSRs between Euston and Crewe from May 1966, the start of the new service, until August 1967.

My responsibilities at first were for planning the annual relaying programme, negotiating possessions,

and arranging with the CCE's office for the various machines involved. The programme actually consisted not only relaying with CWR, but some jointed relaying on secondary routes, rerailing where the rails had worn beyond acceptable limits, and of course S&C relaying and part relaying where components needed replacing. In addition, there were sections of reballasting, where the ballast needed replacing with clean, fresh ballast, and formation renewal where the track formation had failed completely. The latter was a major task, resource intensive, expensive and time consuming. Ballast had to be ordered and spoil wagons were a critical resource. Then, of course, there were the track maintenance machines, tampers and trackliners, which were used mostly on weeknights, but also at weekends if not required in support of relaying. Finally, there were the occasional possessions for the works department for bridgeworks, renewal of level crossings, repairs to platform walls and copings, or a variety of repairs that affected track stability or access.

The renewal programme for the year started two years previously. Each PW Inspector (PWI) knew his section, and put proposal forms in for each item of

work where the track needed replacement or remedial attention. Softwood sleepers were usually the determinant for renewal, but occasionally rail weight gave cause for concern. The gangs were badly depleted nearer London and there were limits to what the PWI could do. The LM had no Area Civil Engineers, but at this point on other Regions they would assess and comment on the proposals. The proposals were copied from the DCE to the Divisional Manager to ensure that there were no plans to close or modify the track layout. Then they were inspected by the CCE or his assistant, the PW Engineer and the DCE together with the PWI and myself. Priorities were agreed. The proposal was usually agreed for the year in question, and it was not often that a proposal was marked down. Category S was introduced to cover work that was needed in emergency – often where sleeper or ballast conditions had deteriorated rapidly. The annual programme was drum-tight since there was usually enough new work agreed for 15 months, but work lost from the previous year also had to be programmed in, and the DCE had to decide what to hold over to the year beyond.

The occasion was a bank slip at Hendon. Here a piled wall is being driven to prevent slippage impacting on the alignment of the tracks. The slipped spoil was removed afterwards. The Dalmag is firing away with the piston about to fall.

The resulting programme determined where the speed restrictions would be imposed and when. A complicated process became far more complicated with the presence of the Electric Traction Engineer's organisation, which had a programme of OLE inspections to programme in with our possessions. Almost all possessions required electrical isolation, effected by a member of the ETE staff. I remember only one incident in an otherwise impeccable safety record, when relaying the S&C north of Bletchley station between the fast and slow lines at that time. As the jib of the 15 ton rail crane was raised, there was a crack and a flash as the OLE was short-circuited, since a length of fast line contact wire was anchored across the working area and had been overlooked.

Then the Chief Signal and Telecommunications Engineer (CS&TE: the S&T were known in the trade as 'the sick and tired') programmed his work on the basis of the p.way programme. The effect was to remove any flexibility from the programme, which had been essential in accommodating extra or urgent work. The whole situation got worse in 1967, when the Chief Operating Manager (COM) decided that possessions should finish by 16.00. It had been discovered that one fifth of the week's journeys occurred on Sunday evening. One could hardly argue with that. In fact, if three-shift working was required, it had to be agreed at the annual meeting with the COM. The effect of reduced possession times was that the depth of formation renewal was reduced and lengths of reballasting were reduced, but in fact the amount of work carried out on the third shift was relatively little. Weekend work was carried out on a voluntary basis, but the favourite shift was Saturday midnight to 08.00 Sunday. That, after six hours sleep, left time for gardening, etc, and work on Monday morning. The Sunday night shift did not attract many volunteers, and was occupied by destressing, unloading ballast and tamping.

A further complication was the introduction of long two track possessions, in which all three engineering departments carried out their work over the section. This led to the creation of 'The Person in charge of the Possession', or PICOP, the nominated person who was ultimately responsible for taking, administering and giving up possession of the line. Nobody was allowed to enter the possession to carry out work without the PICOP's permission. Predictably, it led to the PICOP seeking assurance from each inspector that his work was complete and the road safe, and being told that 'We're just clearing now', only for the first driver through finding that it wasn't quite. Equally predictably, far

Above and opposite. Concrete slab track was discussed as a concept in the early 1970s, and later an experimental length was laid at Duffield. Here are two views of the section as laid and in use. The second shows the transition section from sleepered to slab track. Southbound services have now returned the track on the left, and the concrete slab is returning to nature.

stronger discipline was enforced, with the threat that overrunning possession times would involve naming the culprits! These long possessions were available during weekdays as an experiment. When the first possession was started, between Hemel Hempstead and Tring on the slow lines, I went with some colleagues to see matters for myself. One of the first sights was an up express, running block on block, sailing past a red aspect with an embarrassed driver and a lineside audience. Another was the sight of an electric loco on an up freight on the up fast, going somewhat faster than usual with smoke pouring from several offended axleboxes. The work was going well enough, but the sight of the queue of up expresses convinced me that that the experiment would be short-lived. It was.

I had noticed that a number of posts had been advertised with the endorsement 'This post should be seen as an important step in a civil engineering career'. That this endorsement was considered necessary was proof positive that it wasn't true, and I had taken care to steer well clear of work study involvement. Now I was saddled with a Work Study section, temporarily, for six months as well, and I soon began to realise that work study was simply a way of paying extra cash for much the same level of work, possibly less at times. Men were paid poorly, and deserved better, but any increase was politically prohibitive. Work Study was a devious and very expensive way round this obstacle. It had two components, Method Study and Work Measurement. The first questioned whether the work was necessary at all and if it was being done in the most effective way. This was valuable even if it gave answers that were politically undesirable or impracticable. Measurement was time-consuming, and it was the process of timing activities that caused so much industrial unrest. In order to start the scheme, most of the timings had yet to be established, and so provisional timings were synthesised. These were often so inaccurate that they made nonsense of all that was based on it. Gangs of men worked at much the same rate, yet were achieving spectacular levels of performance consistently which won bonus payments. In addition to the extra wages paid, there was the cost of the work study assessors et al in maintaining this farce. The North Eastern Region had introduced work study without the preliminary method study, and the brighter spirits on-track had carried out the method study instead, using special tools and methods. This enabled very profitable rates of performance to be achieved. Of particular interest was the bridge painting gang. The work of cleaning down bridgework of the accumulated paint, soot, scale and rust took ages and a large number of

possessions. In particular access to the underside of overbridges was difficult. Mechanical aids would have been a great benefit, but little actually changed. Nobody was sufficiently interested. It was of little surprise that usually the whole lot was painted over but the full work value was claimed, with similarly spectacular performance results.

I became part of the inspection team of DCE Leslie Soane, which assessed the relaying proposals for two years ahead as described earlier, in order to note opportunities for remodelling, rationalisation, or even removal. The inspection process was interesting, and the very first visit was to inspect the proposed renewal of the running junction at Tring North, just round the bend beyond the station and arch overbridge. It was the first time that I had been on the track with the new service, and as the first high-visibility vests had just been distributed literally a few days earlier, I wore mine. We had been instructed to wear one when on

track. However, nobody else had remembered but the wisdom of doing so became very quickly apparent to everyone. We walked off the down fast platform through the arch overbridge, but before we had a chance to start examining the north junction, the familiar sound of the lookout man's horns rang out. It was immediately drowned out by a two-tone loco horn and an electric loco shot into view on the down fast. As I recall, it was a Class 85. It was travelling far, far faster than anything I had seen before, and it was on us before we could do very much. As at Euxton, it was my practice to get behind a structure out of the slipstream, and a stanchion supporting the overhead line equipment (OLE) was conveniently close. The train rocketed past the assembled company, after which there was an understandable reluctance to inspect the S&C closely without keeping a wary eye in either direction. We had two lookout men, and the party's discipline in promptly moving clear at

their warning request was improved no end by what we had seen of that first train!

The resulting annual programme of work was drum-tight, but still failed include *all* of the essential tasks. Now and again, something went wrong – a tracklayer (TRM) or ballast cleaner (MABC) broke down, not enough wagons were available for spoil, and so on. Then there was a struggle to recover the lost work. It seems hard to believe now, but as just mentioned it was almost entirely based on voluntary overtime working. Of course as a result the take-home pay of the p.way staff was doubled, and indeed many men would have left otherwise. The p.way clerical section requisitioned the various materials required and hired the plant. That was not including instructions given by the CCE or the BRB CCE. I remember one such, which directed us to recover connections and crossovers that were no longer required for operational or engineering purposes. Hitherto we clipped and padlocked the connections out of use, but there had been an incident elsewhere, and the BR Board HQ at Marylebone, the Kremlin as we called it, rightly decided to remove the potential source of trouble. Therefore we had to remove the switches and replace with plain line, which required the signalling equipment to be removed if it had not already been

removed. The result was at least a dozen extra weekend tasks requiring possessions.

There was a particular problem at Rugby. The S&C required for the connections to Leicester, Peterborough and Leamington had all been renewed as part of the preparatory work for electrification, and the signalling and overhead wiring had followed on behind. Then the branches had been closed, or reduced to freight services only. With the passage of time, the rails in the S&C had worn to relaying weight especially in the main lines, whilst the turnout roads had carried no more than a handful of services before closure. A number of connections had been proposed for relaying, and as it was unthinkable to renew them for one way use, it was intended to remove the connections and plain line them. The result was a fairly explosive reaction from the S&T Dept, who now had contemplate tearing parts of the new interlocking at Rugby power box apart, and the CM&EE's Electric Traction Engineer, who would have to unpick contact wires from non-existent routes. This dilemma continued past my time with the LMR, but I believe it was eventually justified financially on the basis of the considerable recovery cost of non-ferrous scrap.

On another occasion the HMRI (Railway Inspectorate) had concluded

that a Freightliner derailment down country probably had been caused by the LM practice of ballasting CWR in tunnels with small size one inch ballast – obviously known as 'tunnel ballast' – with inadequate lateral resistance. The reason for this practice was that with no space to unload chippings, track maintenance was achieved by fly packing with the small size ballast. The real cause was the design of the bogies then used on the freightliner vehicles, but this was not established clearly at the time. As a result Kilsby and Watford Tunnels had to be reballasted and relaid at short notice. Northchurch, Linslade and Stowe had already been relaid using full size ballast. The problem was that the MABC (Matisa Ballast Cleaner) could not function in tunnels, and so the track had to be lifted and the ballasting carried out by traxcavators. Watford was completed with weekend possessions, but it was decided to tackle Kilsby in a continuous possession with diversions via Northampton. This was a courageous decision considering that the operators were committed to a high speed service, and it was no surprise that with one road completed, the accumulation of delays and conflicts caused the operating department to revert to weekend possessions.

My colleagues and I rarely passed a week without ringing the enemy – the operators – to negotiate another

The lifesaver. The ultrasonic rail detector, which replaced the ineffective Audigauge detector in 1967, and has saved an inestimatable number of lives through rail failure detection since.

possession. How they managed to run the 100 mph service through all this I shudder to think. The GM at Euston (I think), was R.L.E. Lawrence, Bobby Lawrence, and the performance of the service was one of his top priorities – if not the top – and he took no prisoners. Crewe Division shared with us the one 20mph and one 40mph TSR permitted on each of the fast lines, and on one occasion, Crewe imposed a 20mph TSR without checking that we had lifted ours. We hadn't, because a shortage of ballast had resulted in a length of newly laid CWR being inadequately ballasted in hot weather, and the engineer refused to lift the TSR. Lawrence, en route north, hauled Crewe's Assistant DCE down to the platform at Crewe and administered suitably choleric advice. That episode spread across the LM Region within hours.

The fast lines had been relaid north from Willesden, and CWR was extended to the south where appropriate. Hitherto the CWR programme was facilitated by relaying prematurely, and the reusable material was recovered. 60ft rails were cropped to lose the rail ends which had been battered in traffic, and therefore were a risk of cracking or worse. Some of these had been welded into long welded rails (LWR). The remainder were used as service rails in the relaying process. What was now a priority was the relaying of the slow lines with CWR, but in summer 1967 the condition of the fast lines at Willesden was now becoming urgent as the formation was failing. It looked alarming, with white slurry squirting out as the electrics flew through. Bob Roscoe, DCE at Crewe, had a mile of CWR at Hademore which had crept an inch wide to gauge, and these two tasks were the first to end the TSR embargo.

My boss at that time was Harry Sebley, Asst DCE (PW) formerly Asst DE at Northampton. Northampton District's p.way was super for the most part, and it was largely due to his insistence on refusing to accept second best. 'Seb' was one of the old school, a dapper man whose advice was always worth listening to. He once said to me 'My boy, you will only know what was the finest time in your career after you've left it'. There was only one way to carry out a job for Seb – the right way. He hadn't much time for finance and bureaucracy, but I remember his advice especially on lifting TSRs. Most of the p.way management staff were used to inspect and lift TSRs. 'If in doubt, don't' was one of his maxims. Another was 'Always remember that someone's wife and children will be on the next train.' He was a serious man, but in the privacy of his office he could appreciate the funny side of human frailty. There was a lot of the latter about. The first TSR allocated to me to be lifted was at Sandridge on the up slow, and with the Asst. Chief P Way Inspector, Harry Nicholson, I checked cross levels every

four sleepers, and watched trains over the length, looking for vertical movement, which would indicate a need for further tamping, all as advised by Seb. It was fine. 'I don't mean to be funny, Guv'nor' said Harry, 'But follow me.' The track north of the relaying TSR had much worse cross-levels than the newly relaid track.

Financial discipline had been visited on the railway by the good Doctor, and the CCE's budgetary control system had been substantially rebuilt so that progress was reported not by yardage, but by cost. That meant that the contents of the relaying programme had to be costed and reported every four weeks, and the expenditure of next year's budget had to be declared over 13 four weekly periods. Worse still, it was not simple financial reporting. The CCE's new finance section had introduced that form of torture beloved of the finance world, capital and revenue expenditure. The proportions attributable to maintenance (revenue) and betterment (capital) in each item of renewal, p.way, bridgeworks or general had been estimated, and I had to report progress on both budgets as well as total expenditure.

I was not best pleased to find that this particular millstone had been placed round my neck! It had been a case of everyone else taking three paces back! A senior colleague advised me that the one who understands how the finance works knows how the organisation works. I recalled Freddie Fawcett years earlier looking at a mile of wrecked track behind a derailed parcels train and saying gloomily 'I suppose this has to be charged to signalbox painting'. I began to see why. It would have helped if the attribution of capital and revenue had been logical, but it wasn't. The Assistant Chief Clerk dealt with the budget, and we worked together to build up the new 1967 budget, which by now was based on the financial year with 13 four weekly periods rather than the calendar year. One of the skills in budgeting was forecasting when expenditure would be incurred, easy enough when the tasks were programmed, but when the block provision of expenditure was to meet contingencies such as derailments, it was pure guesswork. I put a quarter of the budgeted sum in the four-weekly periods 3,6,9 and 13, and curiously we had a derailment in each of the first three. Things were rather tense in the last four weeks! Running the DCE's budget gradually taught me a great deal about how the department operated, and more importantly, how to work it to the Division's advantage.

DCE Leslie Soane was very different from FF. A fair boss, he had the unfortunate habit of commenting without considering the consequences. On one relaying inspection north of Luton he announced that he didn't think much of the top and line of the up fast.

The PW Inspector replied diplomatically that actually it was the down fast that he had proposed for renewal! On another occasion around lunchtime, Leslie came into the office looking for a colleague who had gone out. He noticed a chap working on a new S&C layout for Dalston West junction, and peered at the design. He didn't think much of the timbering – the layout of S&C timbers to support each running rail at around 30ins – and said so. The draughtsman replied that his instructions were to replicate the existing BH layout in FB and retain the existing timbering as far as possible. A wise man would have left it there, but Leslie pressed on. He didn't think much of the existing timbering either. On studying the 1940s plan for the existing junction, on the title block, as surely as night follows day, were the initials of the draughtsman, LJS. Leslie J Soane. The office enjoyed that one.

The Division received ballast from down country, probably Penmaenmawr or Leicestershire, both granite sources. We also received Peak Forest limestone, but this was very poor for main line ballasting. Ballast needed considerable strength and high abrasion resistance, especially in wet conditions, and the performance of limestone was vastly inferior. This fundamental point had not been communicated to the new Board members, who insisted that the CCEs purchase limestone, which was cheaper to quarry and crush. Limestone is variable in quality, from the attractive but soft Mendip and Devon limestones to the harder Yorkshire 'black' limestone, but even the latter was inadequate. Nevertheless, our new DCE Philip Rees insisted on using granite, rightly so. The evidence of failed limestone, slurrying up at wet patches where drainage had proved inadequate, was all around us.

The advent of CWR promised to extend rail life significantly. Rail weight is surprisingly proportional to rail depth, and periodic checks showed that despite the greatly increased train speeds and numbers, wear had reduced on straight track. Hitherto, softwood sleepers, often railjoints and rail weight had been critical in defining track life, but CWR had eliminated about 85-90% of railjoints, dramatically reducing the number of rail end failures. Samples of rail depth suggested that even with greatly increased levels of service and speed, rail life of 20 years or so was a reasonable expectation – so long as other considerations did not intervene. Sidewear of the rail head was more common, since many curves were canted for 70-75mph equilibrium speeds, which meant that at 100mph the wheelsets pressed against the high rail. Weedon was a bad place, approached on easy grades in both directions, with 1½ miles of continuous reverse curves. The PSR was 90mph if my memory is correct, and perhaps unusually, it rode very well, even at excessive speeds. The absolute limit was reached when the angle of the gauge face reached 26 degrees from the vertical axis, which allowed the wheelset to climb on to the railhead. If sidewear approached 20 degrees on fast lines it was time for rerailing. The Rugby PW Inspector submitted a rerailing proposal when the sidewear reached 17-19 degrees over long lengths, and after careful consideration, it was decided to renew. It was now a 100mph railway and there was no point in taking chances. A rogue wagon, hunting wildly, might have enough energy to mount the high rail. The previous practice was to transpose rails or turn them end for end, but now we were in a different world.

A spell looking after structures followed, interestingly including St.Pancras station. The works department of the Division was monumentally inefficient and expensive. New door and window frames were made in the workshops at such a cost that it would have been cheaper to send the staff on holiday, buy factory made

items and save the wood! Relay rooms and track section cabins (for OLE) were specified in hardwood, and cost a fortune. As for the tunnel repairs, I calculated that each square foot of replacement brickwork cost £68 (at 1968 prices), since the amount completed each weekend possession, trains, scaffolding et al, was about two square yards. However, no amount of protest achieved anything.

It was very interesting examining St.Pancras station with the Works Inspector, who knew the building well. Fundamentally it was sound, but the relatively flamboyant nature of this wonderful building meant that a lot of the decorative features had seen better days, and the railway industry did not have some of the skills necessary to maintain them, nor the money. For example, higher on the hotel building there was a lot of elaborate zinc scrollwork, which had been reduced almost to lace with decades of pollution. Whilst trying to establish exactly what we could do, it was discovered that the boarding to the roof of the magnificent

clock tower was rotting, and a scheme was produced for replacement boarding and protective cladding. The tower was scaffolded, and work was about to start when the (then) GLC's Historic Buildings department intervened. Their office was exactly opposite St.Pancras, and they had been watching progress with the work.

A familiar dispute started. The GLC advised us that as St.Pancras was a listed historic building, *they* would decide what was to be done. BR replied that they would comply, but the additional cost of the GLC's scheme should be met by the GLC. Stalemate. Authority without responsibility. The argument raged on at progressively more senior levels, and time ticked by, during which scaffold hire continued at £45,000 per annum. The scaffolding was quite something, and access to the clock tower itself involved climbing a ladder from the room below the clock chamber, leaning outwards over Euston Road some 150ft below. I doubt an H&SAW inspector would have even considered it. I certainly didn't! The dispute was still in hand when I moved on to track maintenance.

Track maintenance was a difficult task, the hardest part being working through others. This was an introduction to responsibility for the safety of the line – to one's senior, as a DCE or even as a CCE. That responsibility is discharged through staff on-track, many of whom are not motivated to achieve high standards. To put it more bluntly, a mistake by an inattentive ganger or patrolman can in extremis, cause a DCE to lose his job. There were one or two occasions when it did! Therefore one needed and still no doubt needs to put procedures in place to forestall mistakes. I was to learn just how many there were! At this time BR was moving away from the traditional approach, which vested most of the responsibility for track maintenance in its P. Way Inspectors, gangers and their staffs. For many DEs, the Chief P. Way Inspector was almost as important as the DE's assistant. With the creation of Divisions, the gradual introduction of Area Civil Engineers replaced the inspector structure, as professional engineers replaced artisans. We had changed into a railway with a different emphasis on financial control, using machines for relaying and maintenance more and more, and it was high time the organisation changed. Unfortunately, that change was strung out over five years or more, during which the two systems coexisted, not always happily.

There were a number of track problems. The biggest and most serious was the state of the WCML, of which the Euston-Brinklow section was ours. The basic problem was that the track installed for the new electric railway was simply not good enough in many places. There was a general inadequacy about the track structure that was being

Above and opposite. Weaver Junction was the point at which the Liverpool route left the Euston-Glasgow main line. On a fast section, it was necessary to design the S&C for relatively high speeds single lead, in the up fast with the left-hand switch in its normal position. This was one of the very long leads at Weaver Junction, allowing converging speeds of 70mph in the 1960s. Here one can see the shape of the planed switch rail, which fitted closely against the stock rail. Because of the switch length, there are two additional drives from the point motor. In the foreground is an example of the T bolt and clip fastening, which was little short of useless on heavily used main lines, with clips prone to failure and impossible to keep tight.

ruthlessly exposed by the Class 85 and 86 electric locos which were operating almost all services. These seemed to be fine machines and far more widely used than the prototype Class 81-84 locos. The 86s were very rough riders, and there were a number of places that one approached with a degree of apprehension, such as Roade and Hemel Hempstead running junctions. On the up fast in fact all S&C and wet patches rode badly, and there weren't many miles of relatively smooth running in between.

On two successive days with meetings at Crewe, I travelled in the cab, and on the second day the loco was, unusually, a Class 84, E3044 if I remember correctly. I had never found one on trains that I used, so out of curiosity, I joined the driver for the run to London. The riding was so astonishingly different that one could be excused for thinking that the runs were on two different railways. The reason for the disparity in riding was that the first five classes were fitted with flexible drives, which enabled the traction motors to be bogie mounted, but the sixth, Class 86 were not. The flexible drives were said to be regarded by the CMEE as an unnecessary expense both in first cost and continuing maintenance, but the BTC CCE had ruled that unsprung weight should be kept to minimum for express locomotives intended to run at 100mph. Subsequently tests using an early pattern load measuring baseplate had suggested that flexible drives made very little difference, and therefore they were excluded from the design of Class 86, which had axle-hung motors. A colleague in the Research Dept told me of an amusing tale about the tests with the load measuring baseplate at Heald Green. Among the locos tested was a Deltic, and also an EMU from the GE. This particular unit had been equipped specially with regeared power bogies to allow running at 100mph, but on the tests it would only reach 75mph safely. On examination, it was found to have normal power bogies, having been to Ilford for a periodic examination and bogie change. Where had the special bogies gone? Before they could be traced, the answer came fairly quickly, as a driver was caught travelling at 100mph on the Clacton service!

Subsequently the baseplate was found to deliver incorrect results, and with a revised MK II baseplate design, flexible drives were found to make a significant difference. By that time, the horse had bolted and 100 Class 86s were hammering the WCML into the ground. I believe the CCE was about to limit the Class 86 to 80 mph but for a plea from the GM that it would destroy his service. Just after I had left the LMR, tests were carried out using a modified Class 86 E3173, which had four sets of three large secondary helical springs modifying the riding of the bogies,

universally christened Zebedee. The Mk II load measuring baseplate was placed at a railjoint with ½in disparity at Cheddington. The test train ran at various speeds, culminating in about 130mph. A good friend rang me with the news that at 130mph, the rail end impact was 68tons per axle!

There was no experience on BR that would have indicated what was required on the WCML at the planning stage to cope with high speed and a greater service frequency. Whether any research had been undertaken with those who had, I could not say. I doubt it very much. What was patently clear was that the first 46 miles of the WCML absorbed from the old London District, south of Bletchley, had to be completed in far too short a time. The route had been flooded with concrete sleepers with a forecast life of 60 years, four times that of softwood, but while concrete sleepers were fine, they weighed 0.6 tons each and needed 12ins of clean well drained ballast underneath to cope with 100 mph traffic. By the 1980s, I believe that the depth of clean ballast for 100mph plus

running had grown to 15ins. There seemed to have been no great concern at senior level of the importance of drainage and ballast depth in its effect on track alignment, at least not when the WCML CWR programme was under way.

As an example of the inadequacy of ballasting and drainage, the up fast from Kings Langley to Watford Tunnel, as fast a section as any, had 2ins of fresh ballast beneath the concrete sleepers, on top of slurried chalk. The down fast was better, with jarrah hardwood sleepers and 4ins ballast. The 6ft drain was dry. There were serious deficiencies in the formation over many sections, due mainly to the lack of ballast, resulting in patch after patch of white wet limestone slurry. The danger here was that the sleepers were rarely supported evenly, and cross-levels under load could vary by more than the 1 in 300 maximum permitted, a real danger for short wheelbase vehicles. Where the fresh ballast had been limestone, it was breaking up with the abrasion resulting from the frequent and heavy impacts

from the Class 86s. There was a particularly ugly patch at Bushey on the fast lines. On investigation this was seen to have been caused by the track drainage being severed during the reconstruction of the station subway some years before, preventing the water draining away. There was about 6ins of ballast above the concrete beams of the subway, and the impact of an express at full speed was as a hammer on an anvil, grinding the ballast to powder. The sound of a 100mph express on those beams was alarming to say the least if one was in the subway underneath!

As mentioned before, limestone ballast had been introduced at the behest of the acolytes of the Beeching era, being much cheaper and more plentiful than say, Penmaenmawr granite. The problem was exacerbated in my view by use of the Matisa ballast cleaning machine (MABC). An excellent and well designed machine, it had an excavating chain which cut out fouled ballast and spoil down to 9ins below the sleepers, which unfortunately for a significant proportion of the mileage took not only the dirty ballast but most of the compacted material beneath as well. The advantage of the MABC was that little preparation was required before the weekend, whereas hitherto the track had to be 'opened out' under a TSR of 20mph – removal of the surrounding ballast by hand, expensive in resources and cost. The CCE, Arthur Butland, demanded that each MABC should clean three quarters of a mile each weekend, such was the workload.

The result was that the track was often lifted in front of the MBC to reduce the volume of excavated material so that the three quarters of a mile was achieved, but the long term track condition was compromised. The traditional treatment for wet patches was to open out the ballast to allow the water and slurry to drain away. With CWR in warm weather removing the surrounding ballast from up to six sleepers, whatever its inadequacy, was a highly dangerous practice, running the risk of a distortion – a buckle. It took a lot to impress this danger on track staff who had been using this treatment for decades. If the rail temperature was over 75ºF, so far as I recall, the work did not start. The short term answer was, having unloaded fresh ballast adjacently, to hand reballast, i.e. remove the fouled ballast, replace with clean stone, and hand tamp the stone tightly with Kango hammers. It needed good supervision and reliable staff if the work was to be carried out under traffic, otherwise it was safer under a possession.

The use of direct fastenings was a laudable objective, and one of the earliest was the BJB. This fastening was widely used on the WCML, and it involved retention by a screw thread. Screw fastenings never seemed to work satisfactorily in the UK, unlike the Continent. All too often the screw unwound, unloading the rail toe, and failing to retain a precise gauge. The torque wrenches either failed to tighten down, or screwed the whole fastening out of the sleeper, and I remember

getting black looks on an inspection for unscrewing several fastenings by hand. I rode in the cab frequently to assess the state of the track, and it seemed to me that wheelsets needed firm gauge control at speed to prevent hunting. Persistent poor riding, despite tamping and lining, led me to walk through one troublesome section from Hemel Hempstead to Kings Langley, where I discovered that while the alignment was excellent, the fastenings had loosened, allowing intermittent gauge widening of up to an inch over a mile.

Track inspection had become far more dangerous with the speed of electric services, and one had to be extremely vigilant walking around. A 'Place of Safety' meant the lineside cess and not between tracks. The AM10 EMUs (later Class 310) were almost silent. The Watford PW Inspector, Wally Phillips, was a frequent companion since his section was fast, busy, and very short of staff. Those he did have were often immigrants with little grasp of or inclination to use English, and as a result he was often in trouble with poor riding.

Tunnels were particularly dangerous on the WCML since the refuges were only 18ins deep at that time, and despite constant nagging, they were often used to dump old materials rather than carry them out of the tunnel. Later they were deepened at considerable expense. Watford Tunnel was 1 mile 66 yards long and in my view it was folly to walk through while open to traffic at full speed. To shrink back into the refuge while carriage step boards flew past at

Oops! When one of the rolls of steel sheet works loose on a wagon at speed, this can be the result. The additional problems of the 'knitting' above are evident.

124

100mph a little more than a couple of feet away was a sure cure for constipation! One work study assessor, an experienced track man, had to inspect work on the up fast in the tunnel. Bob Nimmo smiled at my concern for his safety, but on his return was ashen. A dynamo belt had broken, flown off its carriage and hit Bob's refuge explosively. He was lucky.

On another occasion I was walking with Wally Phillips through from Berkhamstead to Tring, which meant walking through Northchurch Tunnel, 347 yards. We waited for the down hourly expresses to pass, and with a quiet 15-20 minutes, we walked carefully through on the up fast, facing traffic. About 100 yards from the north end, we heard the two tone horn, and immediately made for the refuge in the down side wall. We had scarcely crossed the down fast when she was past us. If the driver had been late with his horn this book might not have been written.

In November 1967 came the terrible accident at Hither Green, and I would imagine that every civil engineering office on BR reflected on the Southern's shortcomings. 'There but for the Grace of God…' was my reaction and that of my colleagues. The result was the introduction of the Krautkramer and Philips ultrasonic rail flaw detectors within days, well before the HMRI report had been issued. These machines had a VDU and the operator examined the rail using hand held probes. The VDU showed a horizontal trace, and any cracking was shown as a sharp peak. Until that time the height of rail technology was the Audigauge detector. This was a device looking like a walking stick propelling a brick-sized search head, and the operator wore headphones. As the head was moved along the rail, if a fault was detected, a whistle was heard. The operators were often light duty p.way men who for health reasons could not work normally. The Audigauge teams didn't find many failures – say no more than a dozen in a year and usually less.

We took the Krautkramer out to the old Roade Junction, some two miles north of the present Hanslope Junction at the divergence on the main and Northampton lines. It comprised a full set of running crossovers fast to slow and slow to fast, 12 leads, four diamonds and several dozens of railjoints. The Audigauge team had found two small cracks. With the Krautkramer some days later we found 17, some of which were highly dangerous, requiring instant 20mph TSRs. The Audigauge equipment became history in a matter of hours. Later a DMU was converted to carry out ultrasonic rail examination, a very successful improvement. It might be said that for most of the pre-1966 S&C on the WCML rail failure was not so much a case of whether, but when. Boltholes in particular suffered from cracking at 45°, cracks which could propagate very quickly into a complete break, as referred to in Chapter 2. The new system generated a flood of replacement S&C components which caused problems with the suppliers, but the Division was successful in reducing rail failures to cracking rather than breakage.

Most – not all – of the many running junctions at the southern end of the route had been relaid where they stood, usually on a curve, in the standard FB material designed in the early years of nationalisation. This had a weakness in that the rails and assemblies were fastened with tee bolts holding down spring C clips, and screw fastenings. As they nearly always did, the latter unwound allowing the ironwork to loosen, vibrate and lift off the baseplates under traffic. This was a state of affairs not unconnected with the rate of rail failures, the bulk of which were in S&C. The irony was that at the same time that the electric service started, relaying started at Paddington using a new design of S&C incorporating welded joints and cast manganese crossings, secured with reliable spring fastenings, which apart from a few improvements, resolved nearly all of the problems of the previous design. The loosening assemblies suffered from battered or broken bolts intended to maintain the integrity of the track. The bolts nearly all differed in length and once the threads had been hammered they were impossible to change. Organising cutting equipment to remove the old bolts was difficult, ordering replacement bolts was next to impossible. It was easier to order a replacement rail unit, which required a crane and possession, usually on a Friday night.

Maintenance of the S&C was difficult for two reasons, the first being staff shortage, and the second being the danger of working on curved track with 100mph speeds. With a gang of six, for example, at Hemel Hempstead south S&C, four men were required to act as lookout men for safe working (two within sight and sound in each direction and two more, further out, also within sight and sound of the inner lookouts). If a Kango generator was in use (to drive hand held electric tampers) due to the noise of the machine a fifth man was needed to stand by the remaining member of the gang actually working in order to cut out the generator when a train approached. In practice two gangs doubled up to make more effective use of manpower.

We were beginning to find that the on-site electric arc welds in CWR were failing due to cracks developing, and a special programme of examination and classification was implemented. CWR comprised 600, 720 or 900ft rail lengths (long welded rails, LWR) arc welded from 60ft lengths at the various Welding Depots. Once laid, the LWRs were site welded into CWR using portable electric arc welding. This was preferred to the Thermit process used elsewhere. Welds were classified A to D, A being serious and requiring immediate action. This comprised the addition of emergency fishplates screw clamped and not bolted pro tem. Their early removal added to the weeknight workload, cutting out the suspect welds and welding in 15ft replacements. Fortunately, the rate of failure of the Depot and Thermit welds was microscopic, directly contradicting the advice of the Region's Welding Inspector ten years earlier, that arc welding was more reliable than Thermit.

The Thermit process involved enclosing the rail ends in a mould and heating them to white heat. Above the mould was a crucible containing powdered aluminium, iron and carbon: powdered aluminium is highly inflammable, and when ignited the mixture erupts spectacularly and molten steel is formed. This is released into the mould and welds the rail ends together, and when cool the whole assembly is cleaned up. This method of rail welding has been used successfully since the 1960s, and had been used on the Continent for some 50 years beforehand.

Maintenance of plain line was not such a serious matter, but the performance of tampers and liners was poor, largely because a few of the operators were either less effective or less than honest. Tamping and tampers were new, and competence was often a problem. In retrospect what was needed was an effective supervisory system, with authority on site. But of course it was an extra cost that tamped no extra miles, although it would have prevented losing so much mileage in my view. Working unsupervised at night, it was difficult to check work, to check hours worked and even more difficult to check machine failures. The fundamental problem lay in the philosophy that if a job needed doing on the railway, a railwayman should do it. This approach was reaching the end of its shelf life, although it was strongly upheld by the trade unions and as result, railwaymen had to be retrained into a totally different and far more technical role. Some were excellent, many weren't so good. Heavy repairs were carried out by the CMEE, but the CCE had decided to place machine maintenance in the hands of suitably trained operators from the p.way staff, and although most were fine, the Plasser track machines were very complex. It was a counsel of despair, and both repair and maintenance by the manufacturer would have made far better sense. The operators were a very mixed bunch, and productivity was not high.

Now and again there was a malfunction. I remember that one Sunday at Rugby south end the tamper operator set the machine to lift the track to correct level plus, if I remember correctly, 1mm. As I also recall, once the full lift had taken effect, the machine should have been reset to zero lift to

The new railway 1967. High visibility jackets, properly briefed lookout men, and clearly understood 'places of safety'. With the time between sighting a train and getting clear now dramatically shortened, safety was more important than ever.

prevent a progressive increase. This is what the operator failed to do, and the machine *increased the lift by 1mm* with each move forward and the track was lifted 5ins too high before the operator noticed and work stopped. There was no way of lowering track under the wires other than by hand, and a considerable amount of work was necessary by a gang roused from their Sunday afternoon slumbers before the up fast could be returned to traffic late on Sunday night. This was just one of the many strange things that a DCE had to explain to an irate CCE, who no doubt had an even more irate GM to placate.

However, the machines tightened the ballast ('squeeze tamping'), their basic *raison détre*, although they were intended to lift and adjust rail levels as well. When a length of track had been tamped properly, it looked and rode superbly. Where, as mentioned above, there was insufficient ballast, the tamping frequency needed to be increased. Freshly tamped track rode superbly, but the quality of the ride deteriorated with time and weather. Tamping did not and could not overcome the shortcomings of the track formation for more than the short term. Work Study deliberations, based on the assumption that track was suitable for tamping, produced tamping cycles that were often unrealistic. Perhaps 'usually' would have been more accurate. For example, the down fast from Watford to Hemel Hempstead referred to earlier was supposed to be tamped once every two years, but in fact two thirds of that section needed to be tamped four times in that period for reasonably good running.

One of the growing problems was the control of axle loading on freight trains. By chance I was at Rugby when the daily Halewood-Dagenham Ford container train came through, and the deflection of the up fast and the surrounding area was considerable. There is a lot of clay around and under Rugby which made the track deflection very apparent. My enquiries convinced me that at that time, there was no means of controlling the weight of carried containers, and excessive axle loading damaged a weak formation. Alas I didn't manage to take this issue farther.

With all of the problems, one might conclude that not very much was working properly. This was partly due it being my first experience of high speed track maintenance, a powerful learning experience no doubt shared by colleagues at Watford, Birmingham and Crewe. It was also partly due to the searching nature of onerous traffic on an inadequate permanent way. There was a very strong and experienced team of engineers, from the new DCE Philip Rees down, working hard to deal with the problems as they arose, and although we suffered a large number of rail failures and criticism of the riding was rising, safety of the line was maintained and actually improved. We were learning about maintaining a 100mph railway, despite its shortcomings. Such statements are hostages to fortune, and a decade later the LMR had two accidents at Bushey attributable to track quality. Like most Divisions in the urban areas, we were short of staff and a considerable proportion of the staff would hardly have been missed if they left. I

remember that our patrolmen, the first line of defence, between Harrow and Watford were Greek who spoke little English. To this end, I spent a lot of time riding in the cab as mentioned earlier since the behaviour of a heavy vehicle at speed was the best available indicator of track quality, a view somewhat compromised by the rough riding of the Class 86s.

There were a number of regular events during the year. The Matisa Track Recording Trolley (MTRT) paid regular visits and ran at 20mph over the routes in the Division at night under a possession and with a DC electrical isolation. The MTRT was a latter day descendant of Meccano, a clever pre-electronic design for its day again strongly reminiscent of mechanical signalling. It had probes linked to pens on a recording desk, producing traces for gauge, top, line and twist for both rails. Before recording, trolleys were set up fore and aft, and linked to the trolley with bars and recording links. Every so often one of the trolleys hopped off, usually on S&C. There was rarely anything of alarm revealed by the MTRT, although it was useful as a track monitor, and at the time it was the cutting edge of track monitoring technology. It was superseded later by the new BR track recording coach. Ten years or so years later, a colleague arranged for a MTRT, in service on his Division, to be demonstrated for a visiting party of Japanese engineers. He was both amused and embarrassed to receive a letter afterwards, thanking him for getting the ancient machine out of the museum for their entertainment!

Twice a year we had a run with the Track Recording Coach, otherwise known as the whitewash coach. This was one of the LMS inspection saloons, maintained to a high mechanical standard with a Hallade Track Recording machine fixed on a central recording table. Although it could be attached to a service train, it was usually attached to a special train of a few coaches. Before electric traction commenced running at full speed, Class 44 No.D2 HELVELLYN was used to assess the standard of riding at speed. HELVELLYN was permitted to run up to 110mph. The recording gear was connected to two reservoirs with nozzles that discharged on to the four-foot. The Hallade recorder detected excessive changes in curvature, or twist – excessive changes in cross-level that could become dangerous. Excessive curvature triggered blue paint, and excessive twist triggered red paint, usually and unfortunately, on S&C crossing noses which were not giving any trouble. The discharges were accompanied by horn or bell. Those travelling on the saloon were the CCE or his assistant, the DCE, senior staff, and the PW inspector for the relevant section. While the saloon was not a precise instrument, it certainly pointed to places that required attention, and in view of the company present, immediate action followed. Red discharges occurred on almost all S&C and were usually ignored since it was feature of the design, but as we flew north of Wolverton on one occasion, Nobby Clarke, PWI at Blisworth, took his seat. Almost immediately a bell announced a red discharge, and it kept ringing for several miles as the down fast was extensively redecorated in red paint. Nobby arose, aghast, 'My track ain't that bad!'

There were two senior views on whitewash runs. One was that it was a useful check on track quality. The second was that it was an inspection by the CCE and track quality had to be at its best. At London Division we were of the second view, and therefore a preliminary run preceded the CCE inspection. I remember Freddie Fawcett sat at his desk bemoaning the DE's lot. He had a tense relationship with ANB. 'If I propose track for relaying, the Old Man either thinks it's too good for relaying and why did I propose it, or if it's too bad why is it in such a state? You can't *** well win!'

There were the occasional memorable moments on the saloon. A clear run on the WCML was not one of them: on one occasion at Euston the CCE Bill Beatty asked me how I felt the run had been. When I replied that it could have been better, he replied they always could! Bill Beatty was a Northern Irishman with a slightly hesitant manner, but it belied a sure and expert judgment. At one time, the down fast retaining wall adjacent to the west portal of Primrose Hill tunnel had started to move. The BR Property Board, whose role appeared at times to equate to the

Chance card in Monopoly, had sold the land supported by the retaining wall, on which the developer was now building. While the lawyers prepared to do battle over the right of support, action on site was under debate. Bill Beatty inspected the site and directed that 25 or so scrap rails be unloaded at the foot of the wall. Problem solved.

The Midland main line was better, and we had several clear runs between St.Pancras and Oakley. The usual motive power was a Class 45 or 46 with 3-4 coaches and the whitewash coach. On at least one occasion we roared over Sharnbrook summit at 90mph in the down direction. The Midland p.way was much better since the preparatory work before relaying CWR had been carried out fully, and one could get as far as Glendon North before encountering a significant length of poor track. The slow lines of the WCML were not usually tested since the services were all worked by EMUs, and attachment to an AM10 (Class 310) was not allowed, while loco hauled passenger services used the fast lines. The AM10s rode superbly, even over poor track. Cab riding didn't reveal much. So a special train of three coaches plus the whitewash coach hauled by a Class 86 was laid on to run slow line to Rugby, and round the Birmingham loop to Crewe.

Our slows were not in good shape overall, but as we stormed out of Euston, an enormous amount of blue and red paint was being fired on to the track. While this was rightly so, 90mph instead of the overall 75mph PSR made things far worse. I was truly grateful for a check at Northampton, but again the acceleration away towards Rugby was phenomenal. Mercifully, Rugby was not ready for us either, but once we left for Birmingham on 100mph road, the saloon's speedometer shot up to 118mph. The road here is dead straight, the riding superb at this speed. The saloon attendant always seemed to misjudge his timing, and as we crossed into Birmingham Division, he chose serve coffee. Shortly after, we flew through Coventry – PSR 90mph – at 108mph. The gyrations of the coach put the Birmingham DCE Ted Newens on the floor, coffee and all. At New Street, the CCE's PW Engineer remonstrated with the Traction Inspector on E3156. One could sympathise with the latter, having supervised a run perfectly in his view but now being given a rocket by high authority. The electric loco, E3156, was one of the few that I encountered which had a speedometer reading 15mph or so low.

Track maintenance included a number of miscellaneous subjects. Occasionally we had a visit from one of the HMRI's inspectors, and one that fell to me was occasioned by an event in Tring cutting. The old Rule 225 stated that people working on track could lay tools in the six-foot prior to retiring to a place of safety, but they must be placed securely.

A gang supervised by Arthur, whose surname I forget, laid down tools and moved clear, only for a shovel to be caught by the slipstream and carried north some way. This event, since it involved a passenger train, had been reported to the Department of Transport (DTp) and a site inspection was organised. The Inspector appeared at Tring, a Royal Engineers captain, to join the members of the gang. The gallant captain, clad in an immaculate suit, with bowler and tightly rolled umbrella, looked as though he had stepped out of Gieves & Hawkes' window. As such, to the gang, he might have seemed from another planet. We set off to the site with a phalanx of lookout men. As the captain inspected the site, a down express came flying past, followed down the cutting by his bowler hat. Arthur, within a fortnight of retiring, looked at the captain and said: 'I s'pose now we'll have another b****y inquiry into that!' It took several pints and a lunch to pacify the offended captain as a result. It was actually a useful opportunity to lobby on the question of track safety and the use of powerful marker lights. We had lost an experienced ganger some weeks before, because where he was working, the ten-foot between the DC lines and the down fast was full of scrap rails. To avoid the rails he stepped, fatally, into the down fast four foot and the approaching electric locomotive had no marker light. How many lives had been lost before the first headlights came into use?

Another subject was animal infestation. Fortunately Rabbit Societies existed then, which would exterminate not only rabbits but rats, sometimes foxes and other undesirables for a reasonable fee. A farmer near Stanbridgeford complained about fox infestation from the closed line to Dunstable. While I looked for a solution, his Land Agent, brother to Sir Henry Johnson, Chairman of the BRB, rang. When I explained that I was looking for a contractor and funds to deal with it, he asked whether his brother might help. This had been tried before. I agreed that he might as well try, as it might help. Meanwhile, the farmer rang to say that the hunt was meeting in a week or two, and if they could go on the old branch, they might get a fox or two. After all, our fences were very much in the past tense. Again, I agreed. When I rang to find what had happened, the farmer said that he hadn't seen a scene like it. The hunt raised some two dozen foxes, and there were hounds tearing in all directions. We heard no more.

Shortly after, the news came through that I had been successful in applying for a post on Brunel's railway, a very different proposition from life under the wires, and I bid farewell to the railway that had trained me.

The down 'Merseyside Express', hauled by No.46208 PRINCESS HELENA VICTORIA passing Camden shed. This was the last time I saw one of the 'Lizzies' on the main line.

Chapter Six: Engine Riding

There can be few railway engineers or enthusiasts who do not regard riding on the footplate as the ultimate thrill that the railway offers. To do so legally and indeed to be paid for being there seemed to be the best of all worlds, but of course it was not all sunshine and pleasure, especially for those in the Motive Power world in steam days. In my training years, like many others, I often found my way illegally on to the footplate of steam locomotives. One thing that I realised quickly, is that the footplate is a place where danger is immediate and in the steam era, it was usually very hot. My old friend Jim Edwards of the Kings Cross top link laid down the law some years before on SEAGULL: *sit down out of the way, don't interfere, watch what you touch as it's probably hot, mind your feet and keep out of sight at the main stations!* Steam engines were hot and lacking in the level of safety required nowadays, but even with diesel and electric traction proximity to the driver could bring immediate involvement unwittingly in an operational incident such as the well-known SPAD (Signal passed at danger) for example. The benefit to me was that I would find the experience useful later in my career. It was a great pity that legitimate access to the footplate was so restricted and not part of training for graduate and student engineers who would have future responsibility for p.way.

It was difficult to get any feel for what lay beneath with the amount of noise, movement and vibration, and suspension seemed to be a concept rather than a reality on a steam locomotive. My initial reaction was one of surprise that at speed it was often difficult to stand without holding on. There were and probably still are isolated spots where a wet patch or a low joint occurs – referred to by previous generations of PWIs as a 'hole in the road' – which are felt on the footplate. The momentary deflection cannot be more than an inch, but it feels like a foot! I remember one on Stoke Bank, of all places, and at 100 mph the sensation is heart-stopping. I have told the story elsewhere of the occasion when Bill Hoole asked me what I thought of the A4's riding, and I replied that the track felt rough. 'I'll show you what rough track is' said Bill, bearing down on Thirsk at rising 80mph. There was a wet patch under the up main S&C at Thirsk, and I still remember the involuntary sense of horror as GANNET hit it, the feeling that the loco had leapt in the air, and to the sight of two tiny pathetic ribbons of steel stretching ahead. 'Now that's rough track!' he shouted.

As I became more familiar with both engine riding and the GN main line, I began to acquire the railway equivalent of 'sea legs'. Later, working on the District and the Division, senior engineers, using the office footplate pass, were required to ride the main lines annually. I wonder what was made of it, remembering how long it took me to get the feel of the track. As I remember, it was often with ill grace that they returned to the office looking much the worse for wear. If the Old Man had encountered a high mileage Scot or worse it was not to be wondered at. While at St.Pancras I used the pass from St.Pancras to Bedford, but by then the Midland main line was receiving new Type 4 Sulzer diesel locomotives. The ride was of course much smoother and quieter, but on jointed track there was a heavy impact on the rail ends that fairly rattled the teeth. Presumably it rattled the loco as well. The practice of the DE or DCE riding on the footplate or in the cab seemed to die out in the mid-1960s as more scientific methods of track assessment supervened.

One of my great regrets is that I was too late to sample the express steam locomotives of the LM – indeed I was too late to ride on diesel traction on the south end of the WCML as well. A trip on a Big 'Un would have been memorable. The intervening period before electrification saw all express haulage taken over by English Electric Type 4s. The diesels gradually became more reliable, and although they were underpowered, they had the great advantage of not being limited by the fireman's shovel, the condition of the fire or the need for servicing. With a clear road the throttle could be opened, and left open until the permitted speed had been reached, or a delay intervened. With an enormously greater tractive effort and driven wheels half the

On a fine summer evening below Greenholme, a Black Five starts up the 1 in 75 with a down freight, assisted at the rear.

No.46240 CITY OF COVENTRY powers past Camden carriage sidings with a down Birmingham express.

diameter, they also had the advantage of a superior acceleration, which was important given the number of speed restrictions (TSRs) in force at the time. Although the Type 4 diesels were positively elephantine, they were lighter in total than the steam locomotives that they replaced, not having tenders.

On the other hand, at a time of the installation of CWR, they had the annoying habit of running on broadly level track at 65-70mph with heavy loads, a speed at which the BR1 bogies of BR Mk.1 coaches were excited into continuous hunting. It made journeys of any distance over CWR almost intolerable, but resulted in the development of the excellent B4/B5 bogie, if I have remembered its designation correctly. One of the early trial lengths of CWR, usually called a 'Golden Mile', was near Cheddington, and at 70-80mph the LMSR stock immediately started quite violent hunting. At a time when hunting was almost unknown, it was quite alarming. In fact my work at the time involved hardly any travelling down country. There was a debate at the time over the P/D ratio, where P = axle load (in tons) divided by D, wheel diameter (ft). For steam locos it was somewhere between 3 and 3.5, but for diesel traction the P/D was well over 5 and nearer 6. The CCE view was that the ratio had to be restrained since high values increased the track maintenance costs and certainly, in retrospect, the hammering of rail ends and point rails in S&C increased considerably after steam traction. But whatever the ill effects of

the new traction on the permanent way, it had to be accepted. Life had to go on, the railway was changing and my part in it was changing too, from enthusiastic learner and observer to participant. The fascination of steam, which seemed to have a living quality about it, had gone, and now we had machines, dead but reliable – most of the time.

One of my early trips on the WCML was on a Doncaster built Class 85, but it was totally different from any previous experience with Doncaster locomotives – or anything else for that matter. It was very different from 100mph with steam traction, indeed it could hardly have been more different. Moreover it was sustained. The fact that one was travelling so fast was not evident until passing another train. Despite the flexible drive, it was a lively roughish ride. Not long after I travelled down to Crewe in connection with the restoration of preserved A4 SIR NIGEL GRESLEY. It was lively ride, but the moment I remember is as we pulled to a halt alongside the immaculate A4, and hearing the astonished reaction of the driver. He sat, transfixed, for few moments. 'Just look at that! Now that's what I call a real loco. They were never like that when we had to *** well work on them!'

The return journey was also memorable. It was in darkness, and until then all my footplate experience had of course been in daylight. There would have been no point in night riding. It is of course something which drivers do daily, but to me it was a reminder that a considerable mileage over 24 hours is

achieved in darkness. It was without the headlights which are now available, and with what little moonlight there was, running at 100mph in darkness was a revelation. The driver was amused at my attempts to match mentally what I could see with what I remembered of daylight running. The colour light signals were reassuring, but what impressed me deeply was the skill and road knowledge of the driver.

What surprised me was the rapidity with which 100mph seemed to become quite normal, and contrariwise, the time it took for the speedometer to respond to the brake, although the drivers made a brake application on sighting a double yellow ahead, which seemed rather early. One driver explained that at 100mph the immediate concern was to reduce speed, since obviously only two block sections remained to a potential red aspect. He delayed the application, and true, the needle seemed stuck in to 80s almost until the single yellow. Point made. After miles at 100mph, 50mph seemed like strolling. I rode the main lines often, and became familiar with them and the trouble spots, and the general operation of the main line. In my experience, curiously, the riding was usually much worse on the up journey, probably because the bulk of the diamond crossings were on the up fast rather than the down.

On one occasion E3177, as I recall, refused to accelerate away from Crewe, and by Basford Hall rolled slowly to a halt. At the driver's bidding I went back into the loco to check the fuse settings, which were correct, but I noticed some mean-spirited person had included in the design of these locos a translucent fibreglass panel in the roof. I suddenly became aware that, a few feet above, was the live contact wire. Perfectly safe maybe, but the proximity of instant death was alarming to say the least! Another Class 86 was sent out to doublehead us to Euston. On another occasion we were stopped at Willesden on the up fast with a damaged pantograph. In my view, at that time drivers down on the ballast were a liability, since they tended to walk with rather than against the traffic. At that time they rarely used high visibility vests, and as our driver dismounted to inspect the damage, I had to look out for him.

One afternoon when I joined another loco at Coventry, and the driver said 'Take the second man's seat and hold on. The GM Mr Lawrence is on the train and it's more than my life's worth to run in late'. We were running late, but speed picked up rapidly and we dashed through Rugby. As we descended from Kilsby past the M1, we were up to 106-108mph. I looked across at the speedo, but the driver read my mind – 'It's not a rule' he said, 'but we're expected to be at 100 mph alongside the motorway'. It was a very lively ride, especially at Roade and the other running junctions, but we stopped at Euston a few minutes before time. Shortly after having left the LMR I was able to return and ride on a new Class 87, and the quality of ride was as excellent as that of the Class 86 was rough.

On a down run, our progress was impeded by, first an oil tank train, weaving round a stopping service on the down slow, and then a parcels train. It seemed to me, however, that we had too many running junctions for a 100mph railway, mostly about five minutes apart at speed. All too often trains weaved between the fast and slow lines, slowing to 20mph and delaying expresses. Existing S&C was restricted to 20mph or so, difficult to maintain as described earlier and most of the rail failures arose in S&C for that reason. I formulated a proposal to remove half the running junctions, and relay the remaining with faster connections with the new design of S&C with cast crossings. Two things would happen immediately. The number of rail failures would be reduced by at least half, probably nearer two thirds, and weaving could be accomplished at 60-70mph instead of 15-30mph, with less delay to traffic overall. In the longer term, relaying costs for the main line S&C would be halved. Roade was by far the worst layout, sited on varying curvature, undercanted, riding particularly badly on the up fast through the diamonds. Maintenance was dangerous due to the speed of traffic although the sighting distance was fairly good. Here was a good engineering case. The removal of the junctions at Harrow, Hemel Hempstead, Leighton Buzzard, and Wolverton, together with the resiting and remodelling of the remaining junctions as high speed single lead layouts on straight track would have a dramatic effect on the WCML.

The proposal was tentatively put to Fred Walmsley, the Divisional Operating Officer, and I was delighted that he accepted it enthusiastically. It was just what he needed. Indeed it went as far as the Asst GM, T.C.B. Miller, who backed it strongly. The idea of using capital investment to improve the operational railway in this way was still novel, and certainly the quantification of the benefits in financial terms would have taxed the investment planners. But what is the cost benefit in eliminating a rail failure? Hither Green? Bushey? Hatfield? The reaction of the CS&TE and CM&EE was at best unenthusiastic as one would expect, since there was no obvious benefit to them and an enormous amount of hard work. I daresay the resource implications for those departments were difficult if not impossible. The pace of investment in signalling alterations was dictated by the availability of technical resources both in and outside the industry.

The immediate result was the relocation of Roade S&C two miles south on straight track at Hanslope on the principles that I recommended. The improvement in operation, in ride, and reduction in rail failures – indeed in the safety of on-track staff was immediate and marked. I left the LMR at the end of 1969, bound for Brunel's railway, and I am unaware of subsequent progress towards the rationalisation of the West Coast main line. I do know that it took far, far longer than was originally hoped. The problem, like so many others, arose from not having planned a 100mph railway properly before building and running a 100mph service.

Rebuilt Patriot No.45531 SIR FREDERICK HARRISON at Greenholme on the lower slopes climbing to Shap.

My old friend, 42350, working empty stock out of Euston as usual, between the then bridges No.4 and No.5.

PART 2: THE RAILWAY
Chapter Seven: Operation and Performance

To one brought up within earshot of the East Coast main line and knowing that railway very closely, starting work on a different railway was strange, especially working at close quarters. The geography of the system had to be assimilated, the pattern of operation learnt, and even the locomotives recognised. It was a busy railway, especially the West Coast main line which served a rather wider area. In fact it was interesting to compare the two systems. The development of express services and speeds had seen the LNER surpass the GWR in the 1930s, but towards the end of that decade there were clear signs of the LMSR responding with successful developments of their own.

Even the most diehard Gresley enthusiast could not fail to find the appearance and proportions of Sir William's masterpieces deeply impressive – the Big 'Uns. The later addition of large smoke deflectors, sometimes to the detriment of designs, on this occasion proved to be an improvement. Stanier and his successors were successful in their use of smoke deflectors, unlike the LNER, and despite the curiosity of their shape, the rebuilt Royal Scots were improved by the

addition of deflectors. The 'Princess Coronation' Pacifics, often known as 'Duchesses', conveyed an appearance of enormous power at the front, which balanced the huge Belpaire firebox that gave the engines such a broad-shouldered look from the rear. Head on they were magnificent, but the following shot from the rear was every bit as impressive.

Fortunately we have three preserved examples to remind us of the magnificence of days past. Two, DUCHESS OF HAMILTON and CITY OF BIRMINGHAM, are now static, but DUCHESS OF SUTHERLAND is operational at the time of writing. The re-streamlined DUCHESS OF HAMILTON is a magnificent sight, an exceptionally fine work of engineering and painting craftsmanship. It is something that only the most senior ex-railwaymen and enthusiasts can recall in service now and it is good to be able to see the past recreated. I only have the vaguest single recollection of a streamlined Pacific as a small lad, taken on a trip to London stations during the war by my father, but such as it is, only a symphony of rust, filth and neglect remains in the memory. Cleaning did not seem to matter on the post-war

LMSR, at least until the early 1950s. Sir William himself, reputedly, regarded streamlining with disapproval, something flashy dreamed up for publicity purposes. He regarded the non-streamlined quintet 6230-6234 more warmly, as looking like real locomotives. Many of us living away from the LMSR main line met the Big 'Uns in spirit with the splendid Hornby-Dublo model DUCHESS OF ATHOLL and her successors. It is a matter of opinion of course, perhaps coloured by nostalgia, but I feel that the 'speed whiskers' applied to the streamlined locomotives and stock forming the Coronation Scot did not enhance the appearance of the train. Spectacular, yes, aesthetic, perhaps not. Compared with the appearance of Gresley's three streamliners, it came fourth in my view.

Comparison between the two railways was very interesting. There were, superficially, some similarities between the areas served West Coast (WCML) and the East Coast (ECML) while in other respects there were significant differences. The disposition of our industrial areas was predicated by the availability of coal and iron, and looked at from London, although things change, it has an asymmetrical look.

No.46256 SIR WILLIAM STANIER FRS backs out of Euston's platform 1 with the ECS.

No.46225 DUCHESS OF GLOUCESTER in old platform 2 at Euston.

In learning about the old station and its geography, I discovered an ancient stairway to the roof on the down side. It afforded an unusual aspect of the old platform 15, which I used to photograph the 16.30 Euston-Birmingham, headed by Royal Scot No.46156 THE SOUTH WALES BORDERER.

This is a comparison that is being revisited currently in the debate over the proposed future high speed route HS2. Both the East and West Coast routes serve the two major Scottish cities and the counterpart to the ER/NER's South and West Yorkshire traffic is the larger Liverpool-Manchester conurbation. The LMR has little in Cumbria to correspond with the Tyne-Tees industrial area, and commercially there is relatively little north of Preston to compare with what lay to the south. Contrariwise the ER has no counterpart to the Birmingham-West Midlands area, and indeed large areas of the old LNER, especially the old GNR south of Yorkshire and much of the old GER outside London were pastoral rather than industrial.

The two main routes differed in a number of ways. The West Coast had heavy gradients at Grayrigg, Shap and Beattock, while the East Coast was generally flatter and had only Cockburnspath Bank. Both had areas restricted by the mining industry, perhaps more so on the East Coast, but the East Coast suffered speed restrictions at many points. It had a number of fast, easily graded sections, and while much was made of Stoke Bank, the first 160 miles north of Euston had only a few 50mph and 60 mph PSRs. I would estimate that in steam days, Euston-Crewe was about 10 mins faster than Kings Cross-Doncaster.

The old LMSR was a larger railway geographically and commercially than the LNER, but it was slower to react after the First World War to the growing passenger market. The GWR was pre-eminent, with good management and in particular, the good fortune to have had a brilliant and wise CME, G.J. Churchward, who stocked the railway with a range of reliable and economical locomotives and laid the foundations for later designs. The LMSR had no such luck, being created out of three strongly independent companies at Grouping. Operationally and mechanically there was said to be little love between Crewe and Derby, and the new company was not always well served by its CMEs until the arrival of W.A. Stanier from Swindon.

The original Royal Scots were, I think, probably the most successful import from the private locomotive building industry, and despite a dated appearance with a large smokebox and diminutive chimney together with maintenance demands, they ran well with heavy loads and ran a good mileage each year. The inspiration for a powerful 4-6-0 was the GWR Castle, which had acquitted itself very well in comparison with the LNER's A1 Pacific in 1925. Comparative trials were arranged with 5000 LAUNCESTON CASTLE in 1925, and the LMSR authorities were sufficiently impressed to invite the North British Loco Co. to supply the fifty 4-6-0s of similar capacity – the Royal Scots.

However, it was the arrival of Stanier that moved the LMSR up a gear or two, to overtake the GWR and start to compete with the LNER for speed and reliability. The high pressure experimental loco FURY had been successfully rebuilt using the No.2 boiler into an excellent 4-6-0, 6170 BRITISH LEGION, and in 1942 two Jubilees were rebuilt in similar fashion using the Type 2A boiler. Nos.5735 COMET and 5736 PHOENIX were said to be a great success, and with the looming task of heavy boiler work on the Scots, reboilering started in June 1943 with 6103 ROYAL SCOTS FUSILIER, and was completed in March 1955 with 46137 THE PRINCE OF WALES VOLUNTEERS, SOUTH LANCASHIRE. The rebuilding of the two Jubilees was never continued, sadly. The difference in performance and reliability enabled with the type 2A boiler, to judge from the running of 5735, was quite astonishing.

To the enthusiast it seemed odd that by comparison with the LNER, the LMSR by the start of the 1950s only had roughly a quarter of the large express locomotives that one might expect and no large mixed traffic locomotives of comparable size. Certainly the LMSR had a powerful second row, as it were, in the shape of the rebuilt Royal Scot, rebuilt Jubilee and Patriot 4-6-0s, which could match or even better the single blast A3s of the LNER post-war and certainly the steaming seemed to be more reliable. One needed to remember that the more powerful 4-6-0s were not simply a mixed traffic cure-all, but a

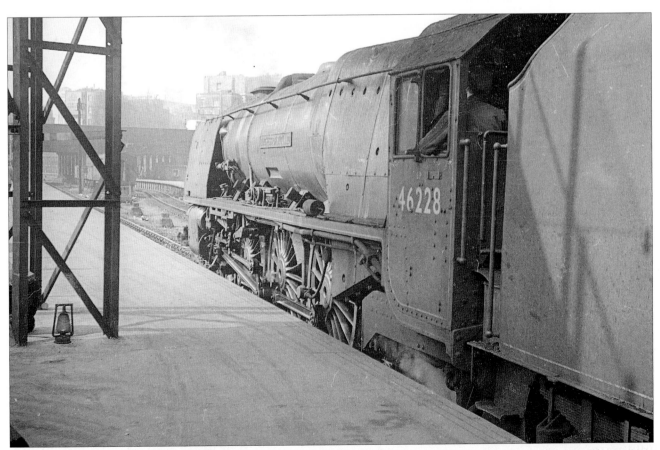

No.46228 DUCHESS OF RUTLAND waits with the 16.30 Birmingham. The following view of a Stanier Pacific was very impressive.

No.46225 DUCHESS OF GLOUCESTER in old platform 2 with an up arrival at Euston.

Rebuilt Patriot No.45530 SIR FRANK REE, not long out of shops, on ECS duties.

Pacific without a trailing truck. The rebuilt Royal Scots, albeit 4-6-0s, were dimensionally similar to the A4 Pacific, but for half an inch cylinder diameter and an inch on the coupled wheel diameter. Within the constraints of a smaller grate and boiler, but with the advantage of a double chimney, the big Stanier 4-6-0s were locomotives capable, if pressed, of excellent running with heavy trains comparable with Pacifics. The 1948 Exchanges were all too brief, but one of the abiding memories was the excellent performance of THE HUSSAR driven by Frank Brooker. They were capable of surprising us, as we are beginning to find out nowadays, if driven hard, which they rarely were down south. The Jubilees and the truly ubiquitous Black Five 4-6-0s worked the lesser duties, and when the occasion demanded, had a good turn of speed.

On the GWR, the system that Stanier had been used to, the CME was responsible for motive power, although in both companies I would imagine that there was usually (but not invariably) consultation between designer and user departments. The Midland arrangement prevailed at Grouping in which the responsibility for motive power was separated from the CME and made jointly responsible to the Operating Superintendent and CME. That arrangement continued on BR beyond the end of steam traction. This had resulted in a substantial fleet of 4-6-0s of various types and vintages, starting with the original Royal Scots. The blame

for that rested with the Chief of Motive Power J. Anderson, a Derby man, who opposed the introduction of Pacifics on no better grounds that he was not prepared to accommodate the consequential cost of longer turntables in his budget. It is interesting to reflect on what might have been, but for the 1939-45 war, since Stanier contemplated improved Pacifics on the principles advocated by André Chapelon, with 300psi, thermic siphons, Houlet superheater elements and a Kylchap exhaust. He also looked ahead to a 6ft 2ins 4-6-4 development on similar lines with greater potential power, anticipating higher speeds and heavier loading. It was a pity that his ambitious plans were frustrated by war, and it sad that his successors opted for mediocrity, perhaps the 9Fs and Britannias apart.

Therefore, whether it was dictated by the existing circumstances inherited by Stanier or his own policy I could not say, but it was hardly surprising that a Swindon man should choose 4-6-0s as the core of his motive power fleet – at least initially. It has been said by many, not always in jest, that the Derby 'small engine' policy was alive and well with the LMSR. My experience of the LM Region convinced me that indeed the Derby policy survived into the 1950s, with the working timetable (WTT) largely based on 4-6-0 operation and the Pacifics kept to the Anglo-Scottish and the principal Liverpool services. It was disappointing to a new boy that, during the day, the Pacifics were less common

than I hoped. The ghost of Anderson still walked the corridors of Euston House!

The Euston-Manchester, Liverpool, Birmingham group of services were almost certainly the most important, commercially, on BR. In the 1980s this service group was the most profitable on BR, with direct costs of about one third of revenue earnt. Their electrification was the major component of the 1955 Modernisation Plan, rightly, ahead of anything on the East Coast.

Early Memories
Like many, I was a reader of C.J. Allen and O.S. Nock on locomotive performance, and so tried my hand at train timing, although often there was work to be done instead on the return journey. I looked forward to experiencing some fine work by the Stanier Pacifics, but rarely found one at the head of the train, and there were times when I laid my note book to one side and turned either to work or the newspaper as we jogged along at 60 mph. Perhaps I had been spoilt by friendship with drivers with a taste for speed. Train timing is something else that has acquired a degree of sophistication undreamt of in the less precise days of wrist watches and the stopwatch, staring out the window for mileposts obscured behind wagons and coaches. Initially, the usual journey north was on the 8.30 to Manchester or 8.50 Birmingham. The former was a big train, very big at times, booked to call

No.46237 CITY OF BRISTOL waits at old platform 1 for her relief crew.

137

The normal view of a Big 'Un. No.46228 DUCHESS OF RUTLAND waits with the 16.30 Birmingham.

Below and opposite. The pride of Upperby, No.46238 CITY OF CARLISLE, at Euston with an express from Cumbria.

No.46257 CITY OF SALFORD coasts over Dillicar troughs with a down Scottish express, taking water before attacking Shap, August 1964.

at the principal stations, and was invariably hauled by a Royal Scot 4-6-0. Speedy and sprightly were two adjectives that would have been quite inappropriate for many of the heavy services of the 1950s that called at all principal stations. The 8.30 Manchester was a good example. It was always well filled – London seemed to get up later in those days and early services took a while to gain good patronage. It loaded very well, and it was only the supreme optimist who would board the train at the last minute and still expect to find a seat for breakfast. However, the 8.30, heavy with frequent station calls, was invariably late by Rugby and later still by Crewe. The trains were not given a clear road as often as they should have been. Also these were days when mail was carried in bags, loaded and unloaded by unenthusiastic post office staff outside the control of BR staff, extending station stops significantly. Hindsight leads us to ask why more parcels trains were not operated, freeing the passenger services of this potential for delay. Strikes by (then) GPO staff may have wrecked the mail service but the absence of mail usually had a very beneficial effect on passenger service punctuality.

The rostered Scot on the 8.30 worked through to Manchester, since LM Pacifics were only allowed between Crewe and Manchester in emergency, or on

running-in turns. I can imagine that the brine workings round Sandbach were a problem, but the usual reason given was the prohibition of the Pacifics from the route from Colwich through Stone and Stoke, and the consequent lack of operational flexibility. As the number of services using the diversionary route through Stone in pre-electric days was few, I never saw the point. Reflecting on the question of route availability, I have to admit to considerable reservations about the CCE's interpretation of weight restrictions. In half a century the means of assessing underline strength has improved, and one can understand the CCE's practice in those days of giving himself the benefit of the considerable margin of error established by bridge assessments, but the general railway interest was not best served by it. There was certainly no evidence of cooperation between departments in order to establish a strategy for rebuilding weak structures so as to clear the line for heavier locomotives.

Even the 8.30 managed a decent sprint now and again, usually before Rugby, but the shorter distance between calls on to Crewe did not encourage heroic running. Twice, with 17 coaches, first hauled by a Royal Scot (46131 THE ROYAL WARWICKSHIRE REGIMENT I think) and then Britannia 70033 CHARLES DICKENS, fresh from

Crewe Works, the 8.30 stalled by the Euston Carriage Sidings signalbox. Neither loco was helped by the banker having dropped off well before the Hampstead Road overbridge, an all-to-frequent practice and only after repeated efforts to restart was the banker summoned to finish the task. After having struggled to Crewe with this load, I would not be surprised if CHARLES DICKENS was sent straight back to works!

For the enthusiasts and engineers the 4-6-0s and Britannias were, however, only supporting acts. The centre of interest was, of course, the Big 'Uns, the Big Lizzies. Turns on which they could be expected were the Royal Scot, Midday Scot and 10.40 Perth, but when working, usually one had to be well down country before their departure times. Initially they were a disappointment for me. Only on one occasion in my first few years did we have a 'Duchess', CITY OF LICHFIELD, on the 8.30 with a huge 17 coach train. This was the first time that I had travelled behind a Big 'Un, hearing for the first time that deep and impressive resounding exhaust reflected from the retaining walls as we climbed to Camden and then gathered speed. My expectations were high. The Pacific had no difficulty with this big train, and I was looking forward to a demonstration of Pacific power, but the load and the

'The Welshman' was a recent addition to the named services on the WCML. Here No.46233 DUCHESS OF SUTHERLAND, in BR days, works the service out of Euston.

schedule demanded little sustained effort. In fact it got a little less and the crew of 46250 were untroubled, it seemed. Happily, later experiences were very different.

There is a great difference between enjoying a fine performance on-train, and seeing a locomotive, particularly an express engine, at full stretch from the lineside. It was some years before I had the memorable experience from the lineside of seeing a Big 'Un being worked hard at speed. In June 1957 while on a survey at Calvert for a new junction between the GC and the Oxford-Bletchley line that was mercifully never built, I travelled home to Bletchley on an 8F with her brake. An engine and brake van was known to some as a 'horse and cart'. In those days, relatively fast services to Euston were few and far between, and I settled down for a longish wait, on the down fast platform.

An up express could be heard some minutes before it appeared from the north. As it rounded the curve from Denbigh Hall, I could see that it was the up Royal Scot, running about half an hour late, with the distinctive headboard on the Big 'Un clearly visible as she approached. It was 46228 DUCHESS OF RUTLAND, and she was going in tremendous style with a big train. The prototype diesels had been working the Scot at the time, and 46228

EUSTON – BIRMINGHAM AREA

I have listed the runs that I recorded to and from the Birmingham area:

Loco	Journey	Load	Miles	Mins	Secs	Av Speed
10201	Rugby - Euston	395	82.30	77	2	64.10
70044	Rugby - Euston	540	82.30	80	46	61.14
46131	Euston – Rugby	435	82.30	95	22	51.78
46160	Euston – Rugby	485	82.30	96	43	51.06
45601	Euston – Coventry	390	94.00	106	25	53.00
10001	Coventry – Euston	360	94.00	94	37	59.61
45703	Coventry – Euston	395	94.00	98	12	57.43
46170	Euston – Birmingham	390	113.00	116	54	58.00
45592	Euston – Birmingham	420	113.00	131	35	51.53
45592	Euston – Birmingham	360	113.00	133	42	50.71
45738	Birmingham – Euston	400	113.00	115	36	58.65
45741	Birmingham – Euston	420	113.00	118	23	57.27
45592	Birmingham – Euston	350	113.00	120	13	56.40
45734+45742	Birmingham – Euston	425	113.00	138	52	48.82

may well have replaced them down country. What lasts in the memory was the speed of the train, and the thunderous roar from the Pacific's chimney as she charged the long rise to Tring. I had never seen anything remotely like it before. A Big 'Un going very hard at speed was sight that we in the south seldom saw, and such sights were to be treasured. The memory remains fresh. The regulator must have been wide open, and the cut-off must have been 30% or more! What was also very impressive, I remember, was that despite obviously being worked very hard at speed, each exhaust beat was clear and distinct. When the preserved Duchesses are worked hard on railtours, one could hear this remarkable sound

once again. It is to be hoped that the preserved Big 'Uns will not be too long away from the main line.

Records of Locomotive Performance
I have grouped my records of loco performances together by route to enable comparison as below. These were recorded between 1954 and 1958. Visits to the Birmingham area bridges entailed using the 8.50 Euston to Birmingham and Wolverhampton service, worked almost entirely by Jubilee 4-6-0s from Bushbury (Wolverhampton) and Camden. Appearance is a matter of taste, but to me the Jubilee is an exceptionally fine handsome locomotive that stands alongside the very best of handsome

No.46239 CITY OF CHESTER is doing well with the Midday Scot on Camden Bank, but the exhaust has obscured much of the train.

'The Welshman' was a recent addition to the named services on the WCML. Here No.46233 DUCHESS OF SUTHERLAND, in BR days, works the service out of Euston.

No.46241 CITY OF EDINBURGH, complete with headboard at speed on the 'Ulster Express' at the old Willesden Junction station.

An immaculate No.46245 CITY OF LONDON waits at Camden loco in June 1964.

steam designs, elegant and well proportioned. Camden worked the 8.50, 45592 INDORE, 45606 FALKLAND ISLANDS, 45676 CODRINGTON and 45688 POLYPHEMUS being the usual power. Bushbury's fleet comprised many of the later batch. The load was 10 coaches, usually well filled and punctuality was probably as good as any group of services on the LM. Occasionally something else took their place, and on one occasion a Scot, No.46170 BRITISH LEGION, worked the 10 coach train, astonishing the station staff and at least one passenger by running into Coventry nine minutes early. Bushbury were unusual in those days in cleaning their Jubilees, although as the 1950s continued the cleanliness of express locomotives generally improved. A lunchtime service brought a well cleaned Bushbury Jubilee into Euston, which was serviced in the small loco yard west of the old station. I remember on one occasion one of Bushbury's few Black Fives, 45405, arriving on time but looking distinctly overheated with her smouldering smokebox door.

Return from the West Midlands was often – as often as I could manage – on the 14.30 from New Street which called at Rugby, and was given an 80 minute timing for the 82.55 miles to Euston. This was usually a Bushbury turn, and I travelled behind most of their Jubilees

over a few years, although it was not always possible to record the performances. Power uphill was circumscribed by the LM's reluctance to fit all of the Jubilees with double chimneys, but downhill they were fleet of foot with a good turn of speed, and what was lacking uphill was made good with fast downhill running. It suggested to me that they were quite comfortable riding locomotives, otherwise drivers would have been less keen to run fast. On the Birminghams, the steady climb out of London was not exactly demanding, but it was not easy enough for a fast start. Likewise the hard pull from Rugby up to Kilsby Tunnel made for a slow start, and times without number we came up the climb from Bletchley to Tring with the speed just too low to keep time. Despite a dash downhill to Watford there was always the fear that emerging from Watford Tunnel, the distant would be on. Oh for a Kylchap exhaust!

On two occasions the engine was one of the diesel prototypes, 10001 and 10201, both running to time or better. The two things that remain in my mind are the then novel sound of these flying lawnmowers and the absence of cinders when looking out of the window! In an era when the petrol engine still ruled, the noise of a big diesel engine was novel, probably without the degree of silencing in later generations, and it

reminded one forcibly of the elderly petrol engined LT buses of my childhood, spluttering and coughing uphill out of London. Another novelty was the powerful acceleration, unlimited by consideration for the fireman's fire. The diesels were clearly in command of the schedule, running in early, a glimpse of the future.

The last of the class, 45742 CONNAUGHT, was one of Bushbury's fleet, and was actually fitted with a double chimney, and presumably a plain double blastpipe. On both the West Coast and the Midland the Jubilees ran fast downhill, and whether CONNAUGHT was superior in that respect was impossible to tell from the trains hauled by her that I used. The double chimney assembly was the one later fitted to 45596 BAHAMAS I believe. Before the 1939-45 war a double Kylchap was fitted to 5684 TRAFALGAR, but it was removed after reports from a locomotive inspector that the locomotive was throwing fire and burning more coal. The loco was probably being worked with a cut-off no shorter than 20% and a partially closed regulator, not unusual with 4-6-0s. The inspector's comments suggest to me that the dimensions of the equipment were quite incorrect for the Jubilee. It was actually designed for the Jubilee at Crewe but a persistent rumour has it that the assembly was used first

No.46245 CITY OF LONDON at Harringay, running to Top Shed for the tour on the GN main line. As Crewe-trained Allan C. Baker wrote in the excellent Irwell Press volume *The Book of the Coronation Pacifics Mk.2*, 'a good time was had by all'. 46245 took the excursion from King's Cross to Doncaster and back, demonstrating to 'those sluggards who needed no fewer than three Pacifics to get the average East Coast train from London to Edinburgh a thing or two that day!

We are now back at Camden MPD with CITY OF LONDON, cleaned to perfection, turning before moving off to King's Cross. It ran other 'Coronation' tours that year, on the LMR, and was the best turned-out Stanier Pacific of that time.

on a Lord Nelson. Unsuccessfully, it seems, on the Nelson, although like President Woodrow Wilson's demise, one might ask of the SR, 'How did they know?' The Nelsons had a very small smokebox, and with a double Kylchap there wasn't room for much else. The only common feature of the two designs was the gauge and the number of wheels. André Chapelon would have been amused at the scant regard for thermodynamic principles. The two rebuilt Jubilees showed what could be achieved potentially and I have no doubt that, even without the bigger 2A boiler, with a properly designed double chimney the Jubilee would have had a lower back pressure and hence extra power, while able to support a higher evaporation rate to give a better margin over schedules.

Apart from the two diesel hauled runs, the outstanding steam performance was behind 70044 EARL HAIG with a big 15 coach 520 ton train. In the 1950s the Britannias were not so numerous in the LM, and were less commonly encountered. They were a good powerful free-steaming engine that had run well on the GE, but preference appeared to be given to the big three cylinder 4-6-0s, although there seemed little to choose between them in practice. Perhaps the Pacific gave the firmer ride, but it would have been a hard ride to judge from comments

elsewhere. On this occasion the Britannia was worked very hard – hammered might have been closer – and could be heard no doubt some miles from the main line. The inviting dip down from Roade saw her accelerate to 80, but for most of the way the speed was in the 60-75 range. The Pacific must have been flat out on the climb to Tring. Breasting Tring summit thunderously at 63, 70044 reached 85 at Kings Langley and 78 at Wembley. The net time was 79 minutes, an average of 62.5mph, a very fine performance and by far the best by a BR standard in my own admittedly limited experience.

With the coming of electrification, as mentioned earlier I was part of a team that surveyed overhead structures on routes in the West Midlands and Trent Valley. This brought much more travelling, largely behind the big 4-6-0s. Punctuality was usually unimpressive, sometimes even worse. My impression was that the delays were caused by checks and TSRs, but there was rarely much of an attempt to regain lost time. That was true for much of BR of course, but there was the occasional fine performance which showed what Stanier's 4-6-0s could do when put to it. As a result I made few notes of the schedules of services used.

For example 46148 THE MANCHESTER REGIMENT with a heavy 475 tons loading ran the 133 miles

from Stafford to Euston in 133 minutes, 126 net. The speed was in the 70s for much of the way, with three maxima of 80mph. The Scots were reputed to be lively riders and many of my runs appeared to be the result of a partially open regulator and 20+% cut-off. Of course one cannot generalise, and the mileage and condition of the individual locomotive would have been critical. Heavy loads seemed to present no particular problem, and after the effort to get up to speed, 60-70mph on the easily graded main line seemed the rule. The 17 slightly smaller rebuilt Patriots such as BUNSEN, HOLYHEAD, ILLUSTRIOUS and PLANET, together with Camden's rebuilt Jubilee 45735 COMET, were everyday sights on the south end of the West Coast main line and were used turn and turn about with the Scots. Quite possibly they were preferred since scarcely a day passed out on the line without seeing most of them. It seemed to me as an observer rather being 'in the know' that drivers were more inclined to run fast with them. The other Jubilee rebuild, No.45736 PHOENIX, was at Crewe North at the time, I believe, and was commonly to be found working south.

The run that stands out is by No.45735 COMET. I had given up hope of catching the evening train from Stafford, but it was still waiting when I reached the platform, having been held

Left. No.46229 DUCHESS OF HAMILTON leaving Euston. Locos starting accelerated hard on the short section downhill under Hampstead Road overbridge to gain as much speed for the mile of 1 in 75 beyond.

Below. No.46225 DUCHESS OF GLOUCESTER leaving Euston on the 'Red Rose'. She is accelerating hard past 'The Bandstand' – the local name for the small fuelling point introduced originally for Nos.10000/1. By 1964 it was out of use for fuelling.

'RUTTERS' - No.46228 DUCHESS OF RUTLAND starts the 16.30 Euston-Birmingham.

for some time. I joined the train at the last minute as the station staff were whistling for the right away, and when the guard came through to apologise for the delay, I gathered that a coach had run hot, and that it had been detached with several lightly loaded coaches off the rear, rather than try to shunt out the one failure in the middle of Stafford station. The few passengers at the rear had been moved up the train. My notes give 14 coaches reduced probably to 11, but I had, and still have no exact idea of the load that remained. It was a long while ago. The sound from the front indicated that the driver was not going to hang around. We left 22 late, and passed Rugby, 51.4 miles, in 44 mins with 70-80 along the Trent Valley route. The Jubilee was being worked very hard, and I remember even now the pleasure of listening to the regular three cylinder exhaust with each beat clear, even at speed.

Once drivers passed the junctions at Rugby the pace was often raised, and I would guess that on this occasion the crew were Camden men. COMET made a rousing climb to Kilsby, after which the train accelerated rapidly down past Weedon touching 92 before Blisworth and a maximum of 93 before Castlethorpe troughs. The minimum at Tring was 67, followed by a tremendous sprint into Euston with 90 at Kings

Langley, cut short by signals at Wembley. Euston was not ready for us, unsurprisingly, and we were checked down the bank into the station, 3 minutes late. The net time was 110 mins, a remarkable average of 72.9 mph.

Curiously, the other Jubilee rebuild, PHOENIX, made a similarly fast but even longer run a few years later. On June 19th 1958, the engine on the afternoon Caledonian, 46240 CITY OF COVENTRY, was replaced at Carlisle by 45736. The 364 tons train restarted 18½ mins late, and the 165.7 miles to Stafford took 164 mins. The stop took only 1½ mins, and the 133.6miles to Euston were run in 114½ mins, arriving only half a minute late. I have found no other details of the run; indeed the load looks to be tare and not gross, and the running times were inclusive of any unspecified delays. The similarity of the two runs gives some idea of the speeds reached in each case.

These were very untypical runs. However it was an interesting demonstration of the fast running that was possible on the West Coast main line *before* electrification, but seldom achieved even when there was every justification for time recovery. A run at this speed would have made history on the East Coast, but it was significantly slower than the finest LM Pacific runs. As with most of BR, drivers were

reluctant as a rule to press their locomotive – and their mate – to recoup delays inflicted by signals. Ironically it is in preservation that we have begun to see what the Stanier 4-6-0 could do when pressed hard as mentioned earlier. We sometimes overlook the fact that footplate crews had their own priorities, especially if arriving later in the evening – the later the arrival home. In steam days there were not that many outer suburban services, and missing the train home was to be avoided if one lived any distance out of Euston. Sometimes less predictable and more frivolous reasons intervened. Often there was a rivalry among certain drivers to achieve the best times or performances, and occasionally a clear road and late running provided the opportunity to achieve something remarkable.

Just now and again one encountered a crew who were prepared to push one of the big 4-6-0s hard. On one occasion in late May 1957 I was working at Crewe Works just after the introduction of the summer timetable, and having finished early, returned to the station to find that in the new summer timetable the Royal Scot no longer called there. Deprived of an opportunity to travel behind a Pacific, I settled for the Lakes Express. The Royal Scot hadn't passed through by 14.42 when we set off. We had 14

The down 10.40 Perth departs from Euston behind No.46228 DUCHESS OF RUTLAND.

Stalled No.46241 CITY OF EDINBURGH (see earlier) rolls the express back into Euston for a second try at Camden bank. This time with the banker still pushing!

coaches, largely short LMS vehicles and empty, hauled by ROYAL SCOT herself, not a good sign. I had at least two earlier runs with 46100 which were quite forgettable, and having started from Crewe, we crossed to the up slow, which was a sure sign that things could only get worse. The notebook was put away and the newspaper unfolded.

As we chugged along, I became aware of a deep exhaust on the up fast, and lo, there was CITY OF BRISTOL with the up Royal Scot, running late, overhauling us. The prototype diesels were often working the train and possibly had failed, who knows. 46237 was pot black, but sailing along with that distinctive purring exhaust of a Big 'Un running well. Her immaculate train was short – 11 on as I recall – and so before long the tail lamp passed us. With my train engine and the Pacific's express bearing the same name I shall refer to numbers for clarity. As she passed by, the semaphore exchange between the fireman of the Big 'Un and 46100 was entertaining, being strongly suggestive of ridicule if not downright obscenity as the 4-6-0 trundled along the up slow. However, a great roar from the chimney of 46100 indicated that the ridicule had struck home, and her driver had risen to the challenge. The sound of a Royal Scot being worked very hard up to speed was as magnificent as it was unusual, and the speed rose steadily. Used to the Gresley three cylinder beat, again I found that the sound of a perfectly even, powerful exhaust was music to the ears. Enjoying the sound for a few minutes, I then noticed the tail lamp of 46237's train coming back into view. Amazingly, despite a load 100 tons or so heavier, we were now overhauling 46237, and coach by coach we progressed until it was neck and neck. 46237's fireman's rowing gestures to his colleagues were comic. I have no idea what was offered in return from 46100. We were neck and neck at 68mph as we hit the troughs at Whitmore, surely an amazing sight and sound, begging to be photographed. Off the troughs, with an exchange of hoots (Stanier's engines didn't whistle) as both trains headed downhill, CITY OF BRISTOL left us for dead, and 46100 resumed her stately progress southwards. A little cameo but exciting and memorable.

Euston – Crewe Runs Recorded

Loco	Journey	Load	Miles	Mins	Secs	Av Speed	Net time	Net av spd
46237	Watford-Crewe*	520	140.55	125	35	67.15	118.75	71.01
46237	Euston – Crewe*	520	158.00	155	22	61.02	142.50	66.53
45592+45606	Euston – Crewe	460	158.00	160	59	58.89	147.00*	64.49
46208	Euston - Crewe	455	158.00	161	9	58.83	147.00*	64.49
46245	Euston - Crewe	490	158.00	164	56	57.48	151.00	62.78
46243	Euston - Crewe	510	158.00	159	44	59.35	153.00*	61.96
46209	Euston - Crewe	490	158.00	168	56	56.12	153.00*	61.96
45055	Euston - Crewe	360	158.00	182	14	52.02	174.00	54.48
46254/45546	Euston - Crewe	500	158.00	189	1	50.15	189.00*	50.16
46256	Euston - Crewe	490	158.00	221	46	42.75	Diverted	
46208	Crewe - Euston	475	158.00	145	36	65.11	137.50	68.95
45256+46237	Crewe - Euston	485	158.00	144	9	65.76	141.00	67.23
46209	Crewe - Euston	470	158.00	153	9	61.90	141.75	66.88
46239	Crewe - Euston	485	158.00	152	15	62.27	146.00	64.93
45676+45680	Crewe - Euston	510	158.00	152	0	62.37	147.00	64.49
46144	Crewe - Euston	490	158.00	162	18	58.41	157.00	60.38
45390+46100	Crewe - Euston	470	158.00	163	7	58.12	157.00	60.38
46201	Crewe - Euston	500	158.00	175	50	53.91	157.00	60.38
46100	Crewe - Euston	480	158.00	175	28	54.03	160.50	59.07
46166	Crewe - Euston	380	158.00	173	31	54.63	168.00	56.43
45247+46250	Crewe - Euston	500	158.00	178	51	53.01	169.50	55.93
46220	Crewe - Euston	560	158.00	178	53	53.00	174.00	54.48
46247	Crewe - Euston	490	158.00	188	23	50.32	183.00	51.80
* Including a Watford stop. NB The first run is also part of the second								

An immaculate No.46245 CITY OF LONDON heads the 10.40 Perth out of Euston amid the chaos of rebuilding.

No.46240 CITY OF COVENTRY pulls out of Euston with a down Birmingham express.

A colleague familiar with the LM's operating suggested to me that if I wanted to experience better running, I should use the 7.55 Liverpool express as far as Crewe, which had a fast timing and was worked by Pacifics. John McCann, who was with the Research Dept at Derby, knew the West Coast well, especially the Liverpool area, and told me later that the train was worked by Edge Hill men. As a good friend at Kings Cross, well known for fast running, hailed from that area, it was not surprising to hear that the Edge Hill top link knew perfectly well how to run hard and fast. John Clay knew of a man known as 'The Ale House Driver' not because of his love of strong drink, but his habit of running in early, before the Lime Street porters had finished their 'refreshments'. Not knowing this at the time, little did I suspect what I might find on the 7.55. Both the 8.30 and the 7.55 suffered strangely from signal checks on the start out to Watford – one would have thought important services such as these would have priority.

My first trip was with a heavy 14 car 520 ton load, well patronised, with 46237 CITY OF BRISTOL. It was a revelation. There was, as far as I can remember, both a restaurant and buffet in the train, increasing its weight. Signals delayed the run to Watford, taking just under 30 mins. From there it was a *tour de force*: we steadily accelerated to Tring, followed by a dash downhill with a maximum of 90 near Cheddington, after which the speed eased back to the 80s. We were badly delayed by signals and a TSR before Rugby, but on the Trent Valley road we reached 90 at Polesworth and again at Madeley before Crewe. 46237 had bettered the 135 minute timing for the 140.55 miles from Watford by 9½ minutes, and had more than regained the time lost south of Watford. I was very impressed, and resolved to use the 7.55 in future.

At the end of the week, working in the Crewe area, I planned to use the up 'Red Rose', 18.15 from Crewe, and waited at platform 3 as the unmistakeable silhouette of the Pacific emerged from under the station bridge. Strangely, it was my new 'friend', 46237 CITY OF BRISTOL, now much cleaner, with 13 BR Mk1 well loaded coaches, 485 tons. There was a slight delay, and to my surprise a Black Five, 45256, backed on as a pilot. The LM seemed to prefer double heading to unbalanced light engine movements. The driver, a small elderly grey haired man, looked less than pleased – the Five's crew were young, the driver probably a passed fireman, who would take charge of the braking and be first into the water troughs. The top link man had been recast into a supporting role, possibly a wet one.

We set off punctually, and as we gathered speed, it was 45256's exhaust, working hard, that was clearly audible.

Her crew seemed keen to get home and as we passed Whitmore seconds early for the first and only time on an impossibly tight booking, there was no easing up. 'Job and Finish' was always a powerful motivator on the railway. After Norton Bridge we were doing 84, and I would guess that on the footplate of 45256 things were getting lively. On the Trent Valley the speed was in the middle 70s much of the way, with 45256 continuing to be worked hard, barking away, only easing off for a signal check at Rugby. I have long since forgotten the schedule to Rugby, but we passed in just under 73 minutes for 75.45 miles.

It was on the hard pull up past Hillmorton to Kilsby that the deep exhaust of CITY OF BRISTOL became much louder than the quicker exhaust beat of the Black Five. I guessed that the senior man had decided that 'if you want to run fast, lad, I'll show you what fast running really is'. Once through the tunnel, we accelerated rapidly down to Weedon at 81, 80 over Roade Junction, and with the Pacific now well into her stride, pushing the pilot hard, before Castlethorpe we reached 92! On the long climb to Tring the two engines were both being worked hard, and speed was in the high 70s, with a minimum at Tring of 72, considerably faster than anything hitherto. Then came a long fast sprint with 90 at Hemel Hempstead and again at Wembley. With an unchecked run into Euston, and an overall time of 144 mins

No.46238 CITY OF CARLISLE stands at platform 1 at Euston.

No.46246 CITY OF MANCHESTER pushes the ECS out of platform 1 at Euston.

9secs, we were almost 11 minutes early on the 155 minute schedule. Our arrival was greeted with disbelief by the station staff and I remember the frantic rush by porters to get to the first class carriages. If the pilot crew had not been on a Five at high speed before, they knew all about it by Euston.

My collection of runs is listed, most on the 7.55 down or the 18.15 Red Rose from Crewe. I enjoyed a number of runs with Pacifics, and the 7.55 never disappointed. There was a keen sense of anticipation as I crossed the departure concourse. I learnt many decades later that the driver of 46245 CITY OF LONDON was none other than Bill Starvis, the driver of KING GEORGE VI on the up Caledonian on its record breaking run. 46243 CITY OF LANCASTER started quietly but once past Tring, reached 95 before Leighton Buzzard. Quite what the conditions were like on the footplate as 46243 shot through the tight single line bore of Linslade Tunnel at a speed scarcely any less, one cannot say, but plenty of coal was blown back over the first coaches.

In steam days signal delays on the approach to Crewe were so commonplace it was almost as if Crewe's signals were fixed. A clear run into the platform was almost unheard of. Even 45534 E TOOTAL BROADHURST with the down Red Rose, allegedly non-stop through Crewe, was forced to cool her heels for five minutes or so. Perhaps the signalmen there had not forgotten CORONATION's precipitate arrival in June 1937 – it seemed so. On the

Western, Bristol Power Box was well known as 'Stopall Junction' since the strategy appeared to be of stopping everything and moving one train at a time. Carefully. They must have learnt from Crewe.

Two runs went badly awry. The first was the first run of the 7.55, now named 'The Lancastrian', on September 16th 1954. 46254 CITY OF STOKE-ON-TRENT, positively gleaming in BR green livery, probably not long out of Crewe Works, with a train of 14 highly polished BR Mk1 coaches, was a sight for sore eyes. The Big 'Un was surrounded by a regiment of bowler hats at Euston. We got away impressively, but at Harrow there was a 20mph TSR from which we hardly recovered any speed. The reason became clear at the Watford stop when 46254 came off having run hot, and unrebuilt Patriot 45546 FLEETWOOD was commandeered off a parcels train on the down slow. I had looked forward to a fine run but I was out of luck this time, as were the LMR operators and the bowler hats. As one might surmise, there was a dense pall of black smoke to the north of Watford that morning as the crew struggled to get 45546 going on her big train. Overall, she did well, but again an extended breakfast was some compensation for the passengers being half an hour late! Quite how a loco in such immaculate condition could run hot in ten miles was a puzzle, but any inquiry would have focussed very closely on her preparation, the functioning of her lubricators and in the replacement of corks to the oil reservoirs

in particular.

The second was on August 27th 1957. 46256 SIR WILLIAM STANIER ran well to Kilsby but Rugby stopped us. A derailed Black Five, 45370, was standing at an odd angle on the Coronation crossover in the Birmingham junction, and indeed had been there since late in the previous evening. SIR WILLIAM was diverted off for a stroll down the branch to Leamington. From there we took the branch to Coventry, and thence to Nuneaton. I doubt that the signalmen at Dunchurch, Warwick, Kenilworth and Gibbet Hill had seen a Big 'Un and 14 shining coaches on the single line very often. It was a strange sight. Today the Pacific's exhaust would be inaudible against the chorus of mobile phones explaining the delay: in the 1950s one accepted the inevitable and had recourse to more toast and coffee.

I was surprised that a Pacific was not always available for such an important duty, arguably one of the most important on the West Coast, and occasionally a brace of Jubilees deputised. On one occasion in each direction on the 7.55 down and Red Rose a pair of Jubilees stood in, and in neither case did it look like a last-minute substitution. The running was excellent on both occasions and the net time for both was an excellent 147 minutes. The pace was generally fast but without high speed maxima that were often features of the 7.55 and Red Rose running.

My few experiences with 'Lizzies' – the Princess Royals – were initially disappointing by comparison with their

Left. No.46245 CITY OF LONDON waits for the 'Right Away' at Euston

Below. No.46254 CITY OF STOKE-ON-TRENT waits at Euston with the 16.30 Birmingham.

Having got the train 'on the swing' No.46245 CITY OF LONDON is opened out on Camden bank.

I had to return to Liverpool on the following day to complete a survey, and somehow 46209 PRINCESS BEATRICE had replaced her sister overnight. She was filthy, black and blowing badly from the middle engine. The signs were not good, and the running was not so good as the day before, although again there were delays, between which the Lizzie ran well. On the up run I was disappointed initially that Edge Hill had sent 46209 back to London again, but at least she sounded much better and the blown gland had been attended to. The start from Crewe was slower and by Rugby 46209 was nine minutes slower than 46208. Once again, clear of Rugby, 46209's driver set about emulating his colleague of the evening before. 46209 was slower to recover speed especially uphill, but having reached 80 after Welton, apart from minima of 71 at Roade, a deafening 71 at Tring and a nominal 76 at Bushey troughs, the speed did not drop below 80 until we passed Queens Park. I noted that our speed at Castlethorpe troughs was 90, at which water was taken: apart from the matter of excessive speed, it required very considerable skill on the part of the fireman to do so successfully – and without injury!

A group of American tourists were in my compartment, and apart from the novelty of travelling by train, they were fascinated at the speed of the train and enquired at intervals as to the speed. At the time passenger trains on American railroads were in decline, so this was a new experience for them. As PRINCESS BEATRICE was driven hard down from Tring and the speed rose into the 90s, excitement was intense. It would have made their holiday complete to have travelled at 100mph on an old British steam train. I made the maximum at Kings Langley 98mph, but this was in an earlier and less accurate age of train timing. The driver had not finished, however, as we raced into London with a maximum of 93 at Wembley. The average from Weedon to Wembley was 82.1 mph. I had been forced to reconsider my opinion of the Princess Royals, at least in the hands of Edge Hill drivers!

Euston – North West
Journeys north of Preston were usually made on heavily loaded expresses serving the north-west as well as Scotland. These services were usually aimed at general rather than the business community, and the schedules were slower. The 10.40 Euston-Perth was hauled by 46244, usually known as 'KG6', and managed to reach Lancaster without exceeding 70mph, touched at three locations, arriving somewhat late. Subsequent trips on the 10.40 were not recorded as the start out to Watford promised a similarly dismal performance. The up run from Blackpool with 46148 THE MANCHESTER REGIMENT was very similar.

later sisters. Returning from a meeting in Glasgow with the Midday Scot, first 46212 DUCHESS OF KENT ran unspectacularly to Carlisle and on to Crewe, where sister 46201 PRINCESS ELIZABETH took over. The running was little better at first, but signal checks put the train further behind time, and some fast running followed. One train which was often worked by a Lizzie was the up Merseyside Express, a big train that included two catering units as I remember. Out on the track it was one of the regular sights, heard clearly well before it hove into view. On one occasion I was surveying near Lichfield, when the sound of an up express brought a pause to proceedings. It was some while before the train appeared, a huge load of 17 coaches hauled by a filthy Lizzie, not making any great speed, but surely audible in adjacent counties, the exhaust strongly suggestive of full regulator and a lengthy cut-off!

The operation of the 7.55 had changed by 1958. The Edge Hill men worked the train with their own Pacifics rather than the Camden engines, and as Edge Hill had only one, if any Big 'Uns, the train engine was usually a Princess Royal. So on June 10th 1958 I was not pleased at finding 46208 PRINCESS HELENA VICTORIA at the head of the Lancastrian. The train ran well although it suffered an unusual amount of delay for an important train that should not have anything very much ahead. The return Red Rose was worked by the same engine, and the running as far as Rugby was fast with speeds in the high 80s at Norton Bridge and Hademore. Clear of Rugby, 46208's driver made a remarkable high speed run, so fast in fact that she was only 1½ mins behind CITY OF BRISTOL and 45256. The average from Weedon to Willesden was 78.2 mph and the minimum at Tring was 63.

The down 'Merseyside Express', hauled by No.46208 PRINCESS HELENA VICTORIA passing Camden shed. This was the last time I saw one of the 'Lizzies' on the main line.

No.46209 PRINCESS BEATRICE thunders up the last hundred yards of Camden bank with an afternoon express.

46201 PRINCESS ELIZABETH at Aberdeen Ferryhill shed in readiness for the Aberdeen-Carlisle leg of the epic Aberdeen Flyer tour from King's Cross to Aberdeen and return to Euston, 2-3 June 1962. Two A4s took it north, 60022 MALLARD to Waverley and then 60004 WILLIAM WHITELAW to Aberdeen from where preserved 49 GORDON HIGHLANDER and J36 0-6-0 65345 took the train around various nooks and crannies. A fourth Pacific, 46200 THE PRINCESS ROYAL, took the train home from Carlisle to Euston.

I have referred to the work of the Princess Royals earlier. In 1960 I had my only trip on the down Royal Scot when steam hauled. 46245 CITY OF LONDON had only nine coaches, 300 tons, and started at 9.05 on a schedule that was inflated to cope with track and electrification work. We passed Crewe in under 177 mins, having lost no less than 31½ mins in delays, half of which was caused by signal checks. The continuation to Carlisle was distinctly lively after Preston with 84 at Garstang, 80 at Milnthorpe and Dillicar, Shap at a minimum of 47 and 88 at Calthwaite. We lost another 23 mins, but still reached Carlisle in 317½ mins, 10½ early, which showed the wisdom of anticipating delay and providing for it.

The return journeys were on an Anglo-Scottish service, but during the summer book the portion from the Lake District attached at Preston was strengthened and ran separately. The two runs with Royal Scots 46116 IRISH GUARDSMAN and 46141 THE NORTH STAFFORDSHIRE REGIMENT were

with the independent portion calling only at Crewe and Watford Junction. With a lighter load than normal, both 4-6-0s were well within their capacity, and with a singular lack of signal checks, 60-75 mph sufficed for punctual running for a pleasant change – indeed I see from my notes that 46141 was 7½ mins BT (before time).

The best run was with 46228 DUCHESS OF RUTLAND. There was always a keen sense of anticipation on seeing that impressive front end coming into the platform at Preston, and an equally keen sense of disappointment at the sight of a 4-6-0, knowing that whatever she could do, it was almost certain that she would not. One lived in hope of an exhilarating performance, and 'Rutters' did not let me down on this occasion. The train was a heavy one of 17 coaches, 560 tons, reduced by a van to 525 tons at Crewe. The running south towards Warrington was restricted, but onwards it was usually faster. The 75.45 miles to Rugby were unhurried and took just under 90 minutes, 78 net of what seemed to be the invariable signal check at Stafford and a TSR at Nuneaton.

As I have

mentioned before, once through Rugby, some drivers took advantage of the fast road to 'turn up the heat' as it were. After a powerful start to Kilsby, we reached 84 before Weedon, and after a minimum of 72 at Roade, 46228 reached 90 before Wolverton. Our sprint was brought to an end with a short 20mph TSR south of Bletchley. It was after the TSR that our driver opened 'Rutters' out, and I remember leaning out of the window listening to the magnificent sound of the Pacific accelerating her big train back up to speed. As we swung into the long curve at Chelmscote Bridge, the speed was rising, and I checked. I could hardly believe the evidence of my own eyes, that we were up to 72mph, and checked again – now 75mph south of Leighton Buzzard! South of Cheddington we reached 79 and that speed was held to the summit at Tring. After this, we reached 87 at Apsley and 84 at Wembley with two signal checks. The time from the Rugby stop was 79 mins 42 secs, 73 mins net, an average of 67.8mph. A remarkable performance, moreover with 525 tons.

On September 5th 1957, arguably the most remarkable performance by a Duchess occurred, certainly post-war. It was, and still is a curious event. I was in the old Bridge Office at Euston at the time, when a colleague rushed in with

Runs Recorded

46245	Euston – Carlisle	300	299.10	317	24	56.54
46244	Euston – Lancaster	500	230.00	285	16	48.38
46148	Blackpool – Euston	475	220.00	290	6	45.50
46212	Glasgow – Carlisle	410	104.00	120	16	51.88
46212	Carlisle – Crewe	500	141.00	166	30	50.81
46116	Preston – Euston	360	210.00	223	45	56.31
46141	Preston – Euston	360	210.00	226	48	55.56
46228	Preston – Euston	560/525	210.00	233	41	53.92

No.46240 CITY OF COVENTRY with a down Birmingham express leaving Euston.

No.46240 CITY OF COVENTRY is opened up on Camden bank with a relief to the 10.40 Perth. Standing by the ECS road watching this demonstration of brute power was always a thrilling experience.

No.46238 CITY OF CARLISLE backs her train out of Euston.

No.46254 CITY OF STOKE-ON-TRENT waits at Euston with the afternoon Birmingham.

No.46245 CITY OF LONDON 'on manoeuvres' again, 9 June 1963. The first 'Big 'Un' to run on the GN main line since the 1948 Exchanges, on a perfect morning, she climbs the last few yards of Holloway bank by the North signalbox.

The RCTS ran 'The Borders Railtour' in 1961. From Leeds to Carlisle, No.46247 CITY OF LIVERPOOL hauled the train, and we were treated to a mighty run on the long 1 in 100 climb to Blea Moor. The Pacific is seen here at Hellifield.

the news that the Caledonian was making a special run, and was running very early. We hurried out to platform 3, where 46244 was just drawing to a halt, *37 minutes* early. Driver Starvis and Fireman Tumelty posed on the front of 46244, but my photographic attempt failed in the gloom of the old station. A crowd of reporters was waiting, so clearly the Publicity Dept had been busy. I remember standing behind a large man, with an aroma of gin, questioning Driver Bill Starvis as to the sort of speeds achieved. He announced himself as 'from the Daily Telegraph'. Bill Starvis, seemingly a man of few words, confessed to having touched 90 once or twice, but having been pressed further on the subject, he thought he might have reached 92. Gin and Tonic was satisfied with this information, but in the light of D.H. Landau's reconstruction of the run quoted right, it was an understatement of astronomical dimensions! Bill Starvis considered 46244 the best of a good batch of Pacifics at Camden.

It was a superb performance, one of the greatest of the steam era. The time of 116 mins net from passing Crewe to Euston illustrates clearly the superior speed potential of the West Coast route. A similar net time from passing Doncaster to Kings Cross would belong to the Deltic era.

Leaving aside the astonishing performance for a moment, any railwayman would have to ask why and exactly what was the objective? The special run must have been authorised at a reasonably senior level, but no arrangement had been made for the run to be recorded, and apart from a brief flash of publicity the following day, nothing happened subsequently – at least not as far as I recall. Certainly operating authority would have been necessary for a clear road from Crewe despite running so far ahead of schedule. There was an unsuccessful venture with the introduction of the Morning Caledonian, but otherwise nothing else happened until the start of dieselisation and work for the 25kV electrification. It demonstrated that there was room for at least a 15 minute cut in the schedule of the Caledonian, but within a few years it was being lengthened in anticipation of speed restrictions for engineering work. Perhaps it was an attempt by someone to draw attention to the potential that still existed with steam. If so they were correct, but in vain, sadly. There was a growing attitude at the top that with diesel traction coming soon any attempt to improve steam operation was a waste of time and money.

THE CALEDONIAN, September 5th 1957

Loco: No.46244 King George VI
Crew: Driver W Starvis, Fireman J Tumilty (Camden)
Load: 8 coaches, 265tons tare, 275 tons gross

Distance (miles)	Location	Schedule (mins)	Running Time (mins)
0	CARLISLE	0	0
12.8	Plumpton	18	13
	Sigs 3mins		
17.9	Penrith	21	21
31.4	Shap summit	39	35
	Sigs Scout Green		
37.0	Tebay	45	40
50	Oxenholme	57	51.5
62.8	Carnforth	68	60
	TSR		
69.1	Lancaster	73	68
80.7	Garstang	83	77
90.1	Preston	93	84.5
105.2	Wigan	114	101.5
117	Warrington	126	112
	Sigs Norton Crossing		
124.8	Weaver Junction	133	121
141	Crewe	148	135
151.4	Whitmore	160	145
160.1	Norton Bridge	167	151
165.4	Stafford	172	155
174.7	Rugeley	181	163
189	Tamworth	193	172.5
201.9	Nuneaton	205	181.5
216.4	Rugby	219	193
239.1	Roade	238	210.25
252.3	Bletchley	249	219
267.3	Tring	262	228.67
281.5	Watford	273	238
293.6	Willesden	283	245.75
299.1	EUSTON	291	253

Net time 242 mins, net av speed 74.16mph.

The 14.10 from Camden rolls into Willesden behind No.46251 CITY OF NOTTINGHAM. At one time the sight of a 'Big 'Un' on anything other than an express or a running-in turn was very unusual down south.

Standing pilot at Upperby very often was, of course, No.46238 CITY OF CARLISLE, in immaculate condition in the summer of 1963.

The Midland Division

Curiously, very little work took me over the Midland lines from St.Pancras until the start of 1957, when I had to survey the sidings of the Settle Lime Co. at Horton-in-Ribblesdale, described earlier. The journey north on the Waverley started behind a Jubilee piloted by a 2P 4-4-0, the latter coming off at Nottingham. Progress to Leeds was very slow, and even slower as far as Skipton. The return journey was similarly uneventful, doubleheaded by a pair of Black Fives. The Midland route was more sharply graded than the West Coast, and therefore involved hard climbing and dashing downhill. The descent from Luton down to Bedford was the high point on the down run, followed by the hard climb to Sharnbrook, although I would not be surprised if the hand of the 2P's driver seemed to hover round the brake handle as the speed rose. It was my first experience of the famous Settle-Carlisle railway, and in the depth of winter the impression of Horton and the intense cold that remained is still vivid. Uphill speeds were quite low but with the snow and general dampness it was not surprising.

Otherwise runs on the Midland were between St. Pancras and Bedford, invariably with a Jubilee. The Midland men seemed more inclined to run fast, with more frequent sharp gradients on the main line, and the dip at Radlett was one location where a high speed burst could be expected. The best was the long descent from Leagrave to the troughs beyond Bedford at Oakley, much the same as Stoke Bank further east, and some drivers enjoyed fast running over this section over the years.

In mid-morning on Shap a northbound ECS/parcels train appeared, often with a Pacific – in this case No.46248 CITY OF LEEDS, climbing past Shap Wells with a good load during 1964.

The Newhaven Car Carrier service climbing Shap behind D290 on 27 March 1964. At the time the Anglo-Scottish services were usually diesel hauled, but the Liverpool, Manchester and Birmingham services were almost completely diesel hauled.

An evening shot at Scout Green, with Class 5 45494 on a down heavy freight, 26 March 1964. The Scout Green signalbox was a feature of many railway photographs, with its leaning chimney. There was something about a signalbox; warm, reasonably quiet yet up to the moment with what was happening on the railway.

Chapter Eight: From Performance to Lineside Photography

An unfitted up freight coasts through Grayrigg behind No.44681 on 25 March 1964.

My trips with the Edge Hill Lizzies were in fact my last steam runs on the Liverpool services as soon after, National Service intervened. My run on the Royal Scot in September 1960 was my last steam run recorded on a service train on the LM. Traction was changing, as was my work, with p way maintenance on London District and then site work on new construction in northwest London. My memories of steam traction changed from on - train to lineside. In the early 1960s with the withdrawal of Gresley and Stanier Pacifics came the first inroads into the finest steam designs, and it became a matter of urgency to secure good photographs of them before too late. Many of the big 4-6-0s had gone from the West Coast main line, especially the rebuilt Scots and many Jubilees. Already a number of the Royal Scots had migrated to the Midland Division and the GC, displaced by diesel traction, and only a few remained. Then came the sad weekend, the last in 1962 when, along with five of Top Shed's best A4s, three of the Big 'Uns, Nos 46227/31/2, the Duchesses of DEVONSHIRE, ATHOLL and MONTROSE were withdrawn.

I carried my camera whilst at work outside, and was able to capture scenes not normally available, even if one had a lineside photographic pass. As the cost of printing increased, colour film, although expensive, became an attractive proposition. To get accurate colour rendering, the exposure was much more critical with colour than B&W. Kodachrome was excellent but desperately slow at 10ASA, and would only stop an express in bright sunlight with a big f2 lens. I used Agfa, at 50ASA, which was much faster, but unless the exposure was spot on, it took a slight magenta bias. Mercifully, now graphics programmes allow the colour balance to be corrected.

Since bright sunlight was as common as sparkling clean locomotives in the 1960s, I moved on to Kodak High Speed Ektachrome, which at 160ASA, would stop anything in reasonable light. As processing was not included in the price, one could control quality, and I used a commercial laboratory which produced excellent work. It had excellent pastel colour rendering, and it had could be used at 320ASA - provided one remembered to tell the laboratory! Later, with a second camera and 85 and 135mm lenses, I often used Gevapan Diadirect, a B&W positive film, which gave the best B&W rendering of compositions that I had seen.

Railtours were a growing phenomenon, and the RCTS in the West Riding were responsible for a number of excellent trips. Two involved Big 'Uns, CITY OF LIVERPOOL and CITY OF HEREFORD. The latter was unremarkable, but "The Borders Railtour" of July 1961 was an epic performance by No.46247. A sight for sore eyes, she ran down light engine to Leeds from Upperby earlier that morning, and took the train from Leeds City to Carlisle. The load was 10 coaches, and a number of people were urging the driver to give us a run to remember over this wonderful railway. It was Sunday, with engineering work beyond Blea Moor, and my elders and betters at Euston had decided that in view of her vast size and weight, No.46247 was limited to 60mph. The presence of a locomotive inspector confirmed that there would be no high jinks even when officialdom's back was turned! The driver didn't see the point for one solitary run, the organisers didn't, and for that matter neither did I. However, he did promise that he would keep to 60 all the way up to Blea Moor. And he did.

It was a steady run to Hellifield, where water was taken, but after Settle Junction, No.46247 was opened out, as mentioned earlier, with spectacular effect. The clear exhaust beats increased, louder and louder as we raced uphill, many of us glued to our stopwatches. Just before Ribblehead we seemed to drop a mph or two, but then recovered to storm across the viaduct and past the summit at a full 60mph. Estimates of power output depend on the accuracy recorded, but for 20 minutes No.46247 was developing some 2,500 IHP peaking at about 2,800, a sustained rather than transitory effort, magnificent to enjoy.

Work on site construction from the early 1960s changed everything, and in place of travelling, I was by the lineside and very much more connected with the business of organising and running engineering trains as part of site work. A year and a half on a tunnel enlargement contract described earlier at Camden brought proximity to the main line, and to Camden MPD. Naturally one walked through the safer areas, such as Camden MPD, of course. Initially I was urged in no uncertain terms to leave the premises, perhaps use of my camera suggesting that I was an unauthorised visitor, but to get from one end of the tunnel to the other, I made it clear that I was not prepared to go by road, like it or not!

After this brief exchange I had no further trouble, but took care not to attract too much interest. This was a time when the large 4-6-0s had been almost displaced by the hordes of English Electric Type 4 diesels, together with the Britannias that were displaced from elsewhere. The Pacifics had lost a lot of their work, but there were many still about. There were few Lizzies about, usually from Edge Hill, and I remember a maroon No.46208 PRINCESS HELENA VICTORIA at the head of the down Merseyside Express one sunny evening, fortunately when I had my camera handy. It was the last I saw in action, although the last one I saw was No.46209 PRINCESS BEATRICE at Camden Shed.

Three, later four Big Lizzies were dumped at Camden, and it was sad to see these great machines now cold and rusting, unwanted. Surely they could have been used elsewhere, but I know very well the accountants' answer - with diesel traction available it was more expensive to continue to use steam traction, even if it was capable of many more miles. Frankly, I didn't, and still don't believe it, but as steam facilities were removed, certainly by the 1970s it had been made true. Once loco crews left the footplate, they didn't very often look back, although I found that later they were always happy to reminisce about the days of steam. A less precipitate conversion to diesel traction, starting earlier, withdrawing the weakest of the steam fleet first, would surely have saved millions. It would have enabled the use of better designs rather than the inadequate and elephantine ones that the British industry came up with as the first phase. I remember the grave concern of the senior civil engineers at the excessive weight of the 1-Co-Co-1s and the damage to common crossings caused by the lengthy bogies. The initial reaction of the LM CCE was to restrict the first English Electric Type 4s to the fast lines between Euston and Bletchley. However, it was too late to veto their use.

It was interesting to look around Camden (on a Sunday) to see the conditions in which men worked for years. "Dickensian" was the adjective that sprang to mind. There was a dead Big Lizzie on the shed road nearest the main line, looking as though the injectors had stalled as she was ready to go down to Euston. The fire had been thrown out heaped round a group of wardrobe lockers used by the staff. It was a cramped site and there was not a lot of room. The track, like that at most MPDs, was desperately bad: one might think that the locos knew their way in and out of the depot regardless of the track!

In the hard winter of 1962/3 English Electric Type 4s were falling like snowflakes, and the Big 'Uns were being pressed into service on the principal services. This was a happy accident for the photographer, although the weather was poor most of the time. The 10.40 Perth, the Midday Scot and some North Country services often reverted back to steam, and on a cold but sunny morning one could make sure that time and place were appropriate for a good photograph. As 1963 progressed the English Electric Type 4s recovered, and the number of steam turns reduced. The Midday Scot in particular was worth watching out for, even if one yearned for a higher film speed to cope with poor light.

Later, moving to Euston Station reconstruction, there were plenty of opportunities to photograph steam around the station. The old glass roof over the arrival platforms was an excellent background for Pacifics, and a North Country service in the early afternoon often brought an Upperby Pacific into Euston. The work of rebuilding Euston gave the opportunity to use locations not normally available around Euston when a promising departure was noted, such as No.46245

Up express passes Grayrigg headed by Class 5 No.44859, 1 August 1964.

CITY OF LONDON one sunny morning on the 10.40 Perth, which I photographed part way up Camden Bank. Two services which were worth watching at the time were the 8.30 and 16.30 Birminghams, which were steam hauled, usually by a Pacific but sometimes by one of the few remaining Royal Scots. Then of course there was the 11.27 parcels, a Pacific and a box van or two, mentioned earlier.

Site work proceeded at various places between Euston and Tring, usually bridges that were raised or rebuilt, which kept me by the lineside, and brought me into contact with Willesden MPD, provider of motive power for engineer's trains. It brought me into contact with Frank Bennett, the Willesden Shedmaster, whose locos powered engineering trains, whose breakdown crane picked up my girders, and who was the keeper of the last three Big 'Uns in the south, as mentioned earlier. One was often on the 17.05 Euston – Blackpool, and it was rewarding sight to see the Pacific gathering speed through the suburbs with a big train. The driver would have been happy even if his fireman wasn't!

In June 9th 1963 a railtour from Kings Cross to Doncaster had been organised, and the motive power was to be a Big Lizzie, an auspicious occasion indeed. The engine was CITY OF LONDON, despatched from Willesden on Friday. The cleaning was being supervised by Harry Phillipson, a Loco Inspector then rejoicing in the new title of Traction Inspector. He had a gang of cleaners buzzing round the immaculate engine, finding bits to clean, such as *behind* the spokes of the wheels! He was in charge of CITY OF LONDON, and had been instructed clearly on his responsibilities. The honour of the West Coast was at stake, and if No.46245 did not run well, Harry should not to bother to come back! On the afternoon of June 8th, she ran to Top Shed, travelling via Willesden and Gospel Oak. It was strange to see this large, gleaming maroon loco creeping round the curve at Harringay, then crossing to the up side via the fortuitously rebuilt Harringay viaduct, and on to Top Shed.

I was unable to travel on the tour, but photographed CITY OF LONDON at the top of Holloway Bank in gloriously sunny weather. On Monday, I asked Harry how it went. The track was good, and when not checked by engineering work, CITY OF LONDON went well. They didn't get a good run up to Stoke, but ran hard down the bank, and according to Harry, the maximum on the speedometer was 112mph. The speedo, to enthusiasts, was an incorrigible liar. A maximum of 95mph hasn't the same appeal as 100mph, although 95% accuracy or better is not bad for an instrument attached to a vibrating and jolting steam locomotive. It was not easy to find a log of the run, but it seems that Harry and CITY OF LONDON had just exceeded 100mph, and the honour of the LM was intact.

I had met Harry during engineering work, and his reminiscences of firing days at Upperby were fascinating. One particular incident remains in my mind, repeated as told to me. Harry's regular mate in the top link was due to retire, and on their last run together, they were working a heavy Euston - Glasgow sleeper from Crewe to Carlisle with a Big 'Un. The driver announced that he was going to have a go at the record over Shap. (*I have long since forgotten what the record for a heavy load was, but let us assume that it was 5 minutes from Tebay to the summit.*) Therefore, once they arrived at the Preston stop, Harry had to "fill up the box". So he worked away, and blacked out the fire by the time the train departed. It was a dry, clear night. Away from Preston, the driver was working the Pacific very hard, and the speed rose higher and higher. North of Carnforth, Harry was firing hard continuously as they took a run at Grayrigg bank. Past Grayrigg, they accelerated strongly through the Lune Valley, the Big 'Un going as hard as possible at the foot of Shap bank. They passed Shap signalbox in 4¾ minutes, setting a new record, and no doubt there were winning smiles on the footplate. Past the summit, Harry could put his shovel down, and they flew downhill to Carlisle. Off the train, they ran back to Upperby, and parked the engine over the ashpits for the disposal

An up freight has been turned into Plumpton goods loop, hauled by Class 5 No.45014, 31 July 1964.

crew. The office clerk came over to Harry, looking for the driver, as he was wanted on the phone.

"He's round the other side of the engine"

"Tell him to come and speak to Control".

When they had finished, they went to the office, and the driver rang Control. Harry could hear the conversation with the Chief Controller quite clearly.

"Are you the driver of the 22.50 Euston - Glasgow?"

"Yes" was the answer.

"I believe this was your last run, wasn't it?"

"Yes".

"Did you have a good run?"

"Yes. We broke the record up Shap for this load. 4¾ minutes"

"That's very good indeed. You must have been going fast. What sort of speed were you doing at Tebay?"

"About 80."

There was a short silence before the voice of the Chief Controller spoke again. *"What about the 20mph temporary speed restriction over the Lune bridge at Tebay?"*

I made two journeys to the Shap area in April and August 1964 to photograph steam traction on heavy gradients in famous locations among moorland scenery before the end came. A priority was to record the Big 'Uns on the banks before too late. In fact they were elusive, and apt to appear when the photographer was unprepared or in the wrong location. Zoom lenses were like standard engines - good for a variety of tasks, but not as good as one designed for a specific task. Carrying screw mounted lenses around with two cameras meant that each shot needed a choice of two lenses, two bodies, and *that both those bodies had not run out of film!*

Diesel traction only appeared on the principal services. The English Electric Type 4s seemed to be used principally between Euston, Birmingham, Liverpool and Manchester. The cavalcade of steam over Shap, Grayrigg and Ais Gill was rewarding, but Britannias, Jubilees and a hundred Black Fives were no substitute for a Big 'Un going full blast. There were a number of extras running in August, most of which were hauled by Black Fives. Two 2-6-4Ts were banking, one of which a Fowler, No.42414, emitted volumes of black exhaust which at least made a good photograph. The standard rule seemed to be to plod along steadily and let the banker do most of the work. Friendly signalmen, particularly at Scout Green, were very helpful with times and trains. Three bankers were at work from Tebay, or Oxenholme on Sundays and on certain Saturday services.

The time spent was well worthwhile and the photography generally successful, but we still lacked the opportunity for an Eric Treacy shot of a Big 'Un thundering up the 1 in 75 with a volcanic exhaust. It was sad to see CITY OF BRISTOL hauling slow freight in the evening, but one of the best sights was old friend DUCHESS OF RUTLAND at speed on a down express at Tebay North. With a slight rattle of the motion and a rapid exhaust the Pacific was taking a fast run at the bank, a reminder of the great days of steam.

Desperate measures were called for, and a small group gathered at Shap Wells on a chilly but clear August Sunday morning at about 6.30am in wait for the overnight expresses. Banking was not available from Tebay on Sundays, but from Oxenholme instead. Using the signalpost telephone to our friend at Scout Green the advice was that two heavily delayed trains were in the Lancaster area. Although bright, my light meter felt that things were not that good, and the film speed required lower speeds and a wide open aperture. Very early morning photography with colour was tricky, and the light was behind a hard-working down train.

After a freezing eternity a cloud of black smoke appeared down in the Lune Valley and a strident exhaust gradually became audible. As it passed Scout Green, the exhaust was from three cylinders, not four. At that moment a Cl. 4MT No.43035 appeared with an engineer's train on the up line, threatening to blank us out, but the God of photographers intervened, and the train halted back in the cutting north of

Fowler 2-6-4 tank No.42414 working hard, banking a down freight at Greenholme on 28 March 1964.

In the familiar surroundings of Ais Gill, just by the overbridge at the summit of the bank, Ivatt 2-6-0 No.43049 reaches the summit with a southbound freight. The 4MT is freshly ex-works, believe it or not, and is a long way from her home depot at Heaton Mersey.

Shap Wells. Jubilee No.45716 SWIFTSURE rounded the bend, eleven coaches on, no banker, roaring exhaust, just about holding her own. A splendid photo. Sadly she was withdrawn a few weeks later.

The Jubilee had just reached the summit, when black smoke appeared down by Scout Green, and we could see the second train in the distance. The train had been checked to little more than walking pace, but at the last minute the signals must have cleared, as the black smoke gave way to grey as the driver opened the regulator. When I saw the size of the train I realised that it must have been a close thing at Scout Green for the driver, managing to keep his big train on the move. Fortunately it was dry and bright, as the Big 'Uns were reputed to be a bit light on their feet in the damp when working hard.

What followed was spectacular in the extreme. As the train rounded the bend, there was the familiar square-shouldered front end, a Big 'Un, with her heavy exhaust beat echoing around the Fells. You could hear her coming! The engine was No.46235 CITY OF

BIRMINGHAM, and she could not have been blacker, which made exposure even more difficult, more like an amorphous black blob, a photographic black hole. She had a big train, 13 sleepers and a BG. The Pacific had been opened right out on the 1 in 75, and with her exhaust quickening, she was actually accelerating her large train steadily despite the 1 in 75 gradient. The coal pusher was at work, as, presumably, was the fireman. The exhaust was thunderous, and the exhaust beats were so heavy that they could be felt through the soles of my shoes as I stood at the trackside. The ground, quite literally, shook as she went past. The four of us listened in silence, spellbound as No.46235 roared up the cutting to the summit, where the engine must have been eased to judge by the sound of the exhaust. As with DUCHESS OF RUTLAND years before, it was an absolutely unforgettable experience. It was the most memorable experience of sheer power that I witnessed in the days of steam.

The weekend finished at Carlisle on August 2nd 1964, joining an up service to Euston from Perth. There at the head

was not a diesel, but No.46254 CITY OF STOKE-ON-TRENT, complete with yellow cab stripe. The schedule was easy and there was no point in timing, although our top speed down from Shap to Oxenholme was about 84 mph, I remember. No.46254 ran through to Crewe, after which an English Electric Type 4 took over for the final stretch to Euston. I took several photos of No. 46254 from the train on the heavy curves in the Penrith area, but the light was going, and we parted from her at Crewe. It was my last run with a Stanier Pacific. Down south, the remaining locomotives had been running too many miles, so I was told, and within a month they had been withdrawn, the end of an era. My last sight was of CITY OF LONDON on August 16th, first running light from Willesden to Euston, and then heading north with the 17.05 to Blackpool. A month later came the last run with a Scot, on a railtour, No.46155 THE LANCER, on September 19th.

It was all over.

The big 4-6-0s, so long a feature of the WCML, were fast disappearing. I was lucky to be at Greenholme when a heavy northbound express appeared from the south. The train loco was Royal Scot No.46160 QUEEN VICTORIA'S RIFLEMAN, and the banker on 26 March 1964 was friend No.42414 once more.

An overnight express, heavily delayed, pounds up to Shap Wells behind No.45716 SWIFTSURE. The Jubilee was condemned two weeks later

One of Crewe's 'Heavenly Twins', rebuilt Jubilee No. 45736 PHOENIX breasts Shap summit with a down parcels service on 26 March 1964.

An up express hauled by a filthy Britannia, No.70008 appropriately named BLACK PRINCE at speed over the troughs at Dillicar.

The driver of No.46228 DUCHESS OF RUTLAND has opened out to attack Shap bank at speed with an Anglo-Scottish relief, 2 August 1964.

No.46254 on a relief to the down Midday Scot clearing the top of Grayrigg bank.

No.70015 APOLLO at Grayrigg on 'The Lakes Express', now reduced to three coaches on 1 August 1964.

An up express climbs smokily away from Penrith past Clifton headed by No.70045 LORD ROWALLAN, 31 July 1964.

Heavy up express passes Grayrigg double headed by the final Jubilee No.45742 CONNAUGHT, piloted by Class 5 No.45055, 1 August 1964.

No.44859 approaches Grayrigg station with an up express.

A relief to the down 'Midday Scot', going well, leans to the curve at Grayrigg Box hauled by No.46254 CITY OF STOKE-ON-TRENT. (Telephoto shot).

The following shot of Jubilee, No.45716 SWIFTSURE, toiling past Shap Wells. Ivatt 4MT 2-6-0 No.43035 simmers quietly on a P.way train, loading spoil.

Epilogue

For just over ten years I was able to be both railway engineer and steam enthusiast, but I could not ignore the desperate state of steam traction as the 1960s progressed. While 1964 marked the end of express steam power, lesser classes continued up to August 1968, usually in appalling condition. It couldn't last much longer, and while steam locos retained that attraction which drew most of us to them, the railway was indeed moving on. It was a relief with diesel, later electric traction, to sit back, read, sleep or talk, rather than try to record the efforts of a poorly maintained steam loco in the hands of a disenchanted crew.

However, it had been a wonderful time, gaining experience in my chosen career, but able to relate it to the railway which so many of us regard with affection. Today the West Coast and Midland main lines are a far cry from the lines that I first saw. The railway and preservation are now at arm's length, necessarily. Evolution had almost petered out with steam, but in the near-half century since, change and improvement has steadily taken us forward. The blue electric locomotives of the early 1960s have long gone, as have most of their successors. What lies ahead? A new high-speed railway, HS2, is planned to relieve the heavily laden main lines. No doubt there will be societies formed to preserve the last Pendolino and Voyager as they too, pass on. But who knows what may emerge in future from Darlington?

Glossary

BTC	British Transport Commission
WR/SR/LMR)	Western/Southern/London Midland/Eastern/North
ER/NER/ScR)	Eastern/Scottish Regions of British Railways
LMSR	London Midland & Scottish Railway (One of the Big Four)
L&B	London & Birmingham Railway
LNWR	London & North Western Railway
L&Y	Lancashire & Yorkshire Railway
GWR	Great Western Railway
WCML	West Coast main line
ECML	East Coast main line
GN	Jargon for the portion of the ECML which was built by the Great Northern Railway
GNOS	Great North of Scotland Railway
NCB	National Coal Board
GM	General Manager
CCE	Chief Civil Engineer
CM&EE	Chief Mechanical & Electrical Engineer
CS&TE	Chief Signal & Telecommunications Engineer
DCE	Divisional Civil Engineer
DE	District Engineer (Civil)
AREB	Area Resident Engineer (Bridges)
PWI	Permanent Way Inspector
S&T	Signals & Telecommunications Dept
C&W	Carriage & Wagon Dept
DOS	District Operating Superintendent
DED	District Electric Depot
AC/DC	Alternating / Direct Current
RT / BT	Right Time / Before Time
HMRI	Her Majesty's Railway Inspectorate
H&SAWA	Health & Safety at Work Act
RC	Reinforced Concrete
PC	Prestressed Concrete
WI	Wrought iron
MS	Mild steel
RSJ	Rolled steel joist
BFB	Broad flange beam
Abutment	Support at each end of a bridge span
Soffit	The underside of a bridge
Spandrel	The walls above the arch ring retaining the in-fill and backing up to road level.
Parapet.	The wall above the spandrel.
Pilaster.	The brick end block at each end of the parapet.
Jack Arches	Arched in-fill between secondary girders
Voussoirs	The ornamental shaped stones forming an arch ring on a bridge/tunnel portal face.
Wing wall	Tapered retaining wall either side of the abutment
Newel	The square brickwork block at the outer ends of the wing walls.
BH	Bullhead (Rail)
FB	Flat Bottom (Rail)
CWR	Continuous Welded Rail
LWR	Long Welded Rail
BJB	Bayliss, Jones & Bayliss: early CWR fastening
SHC	Spring Hoop Clip: early CWR fastening
S&C/P&C	Switches/Points and Crossings
PSR	Permanent Speed Restriction
TSR	Temporary speed restriction
TRM	Track relaying machine
MABC	Matisa automatic ballast cleaner
MTRT	Matisa Track Recording Trolley
Ironwork	General reference to S&C layout
Jarrah	Hardwood used for sleepers. From Australia.
Lead	A set of points. (*Formerly called a half lead*).
Crossover	Two leads of the same hand facing each other between two tracks. (*Formerly called a lead*).
Tandem	One lead overlapping another.
Three Throw	A tandem with the switches at the same point (probably no longer in existence). Used only in goods sidings.
Four throw	As for three throw (almost certainly no longer in existence).
Diamond	One track crossing another.
Single slip	A diamond with a slip road linking the two tracks in one direction.
Double slip	As a single slip but with two slip roads linking both tracks in both directions.
Trap point	A single switch in one rail, sprung, standing open against wrong direction movements.
Road	General reference to track
Formation	The foundation layer below the ballast, including drainage.
Crib	Supporting grid structure, often on site formed of old sleepers.
RB	Series of cranes manufactured by Ruston Bucyrus also used as draglines or excavators
Possession	Legal means of closing track to normal services for a specified period
Twist	Rate of change of level between rails
On the floor	Colourful description of a derailment
Off the road	As above